The State of Science and Research: Some New Indicators

Other Titles in This Series

Technological Innovation: The Experimental R&D Incentives Program, edited by Donald E. Cunningham, John R. Craig, and Theodore Schlie

Federal Funding of Civilian Research and Development, Michael Michaelis, project director and editor

Ceramic Microstructures '76: With Emphasis on Energy Related Application, edited by Richard M. Fulrath and Joseph A. Pask

Westview Special Studies in Science and Technology

The State of Science and Research: Some New Indicators
edited by Nestor E. Terleckyj

A series of important new indicators of the state of science and research in the United States have been developed in this comprehensive volume, which places primary emphasis on developing indicators of the impact of scientific and research activities on the economy and society. One group of indicators concerns the amount of economic growth that, given certain assumptions, can be attributed to industrial research. A second group contains new measures of the level of effort in R&D activities, including an analysis of regional trends in the conduct of R&D by business, government, and academic sectors and in the conduct of privately supported and government-supported R&D over the past ten years. The final section of the volume traces changes in the enrollments in science courses and in the level of the knowledge of science by high school students as determined by standardized achievement tests administered nationally during different years. The indicators presented in this volume suggest that a pervasive and substantial downturn has occurred in American scientific and research activities since the late 1960s and that, as yet, there are no indications of a reversal of this trend.

Nestor E. Terleckyj is the director of the Center for Socio-Economic Analysis of the National Planning Association. He is the author of a number of books and articles on quantitative economics and has previously been assistant director of the Program Evaluation Staff, U.S. Bureau of the Budget, and senior economist of the National Industrial Conference Board Inc., New York City.

The State of Science and Research: Some New Indicators

Nestor E. Terleckyj, Editor

Published for the
National Planning Association
by
Westview Press
Boulder, Colorado

Westview Special Studies in Science and Technology

This book was prepared with the support of National Science Foundation grant number SOC 74-17574. The opinions, findings, and conclusions expressed herein are those of the authors and do not necessarily reflect the views of NSF.

Copyright © 1977 by Westview Press

Published 1977 in the United States of America by
  Westview Press, Inc.
  1898 Flatiron Court
  Boulder, Colorado 80301
  Frederick A. Praeger, Publisher and Editorial Director

Library of Congress Cataloging in Publication Data
Main entry under title:

The State of science and research.

  (Westview special studies in science and technology)
  1. Science—United States—Addresses, essays, lectures. 2. Research—United States—Addresses, essays, lectures. I. Terleckyj, Nestor E.
Q127.U6S7   301.24'3   76-44390
ISBN 0-89158-124-3

Printed and bound in the United States of America

Contents

Acknowledgments

In preparing this study, we had the benefit of consulting assistance from Mr. Thomas Mills who suggested many sources of data and their treatment and reviewed some of the earlier drafts. Comments received from Professor Derek de Solla Price were of great help in revising the chartbook summary of this study and in reviewing our approach to a number of subjects. We would like to thank Messrs. Morris Cobern and George James for their help in obtaining and interpreting statistical information. We also received many helpful comments and suggestions from Messrs. Albert Biderman and Michael Crotty.

Mr. Joseph Schachter, author of Chapter 7 of this work, wishes to express his appreciation to Messrs. Francisco Bayo and Richard Foster for providing the life tables which form the basis of his analysis on "Medical Advances and Life Expectancy, 1940-70." He would also like to thank Mr. Daniel Mullally for advice concerning recent medical advances, Mr. Thomas N. E. Greville for instruction on the actuarial principles implicit in the hypothesis, and Messrs. Robert Armstrong and Michael Zugzda and their staffs for making available the necessary mortality statistics and offering advice on their proper adjustment. Mr. Schachter also appreciates the permission granted by the American Medical Association to reproduce extensively from its copyrighted materials on the significant medical advances included in Appendix A of Chapter 7.

The present work was supported by research grant SOC 74-17574 A01 from the National Science Foundation, but the opinions, findings and conclusions or recommendations expressed herein are those of the authors of the individual chapters and do not necessarily reflect the views of NSF.

N.E.T.

About the Authors

EDWIN MANSFIELD is professor of economics at the University of Pennsylvania. He is the author of several basic works in the economics of innovation as well as of numerous other books and articles.

NEIL J. McMULLEN is assistant director of internation studies at the National Planning Association. He was formerly associate professor of economics at the University of Illinois and an economist at the World Bank.

RORY PAREDES is a member of the National Planning Association's research staff. She has participated in numerous studies on economics, manpower analysis and evaluation of public programs in education.

EDWARD L. RHODES is a teaching fellow at the Carnegie-Mellon University and a former member of the research staff at the National Planning Association.

JOSEPH SCHACHTER has held professional positions in the field of statistics and demography with the National Institutes of Health and with the Social Security Administration. He is the author of a number of studies published in statistical and bio-medical journals.

NESTOR E. TERLECKYJ is the director of the Center for Socio-Economic Analysis of the National Planning Association. He is the author of a number of books and articles in quantitative economics and has previously held professional positions in research institutions and government.

IVARS ZAGERIS is currently a member of the research staff of the American Council on Education and was formerly a member of the research staff at the National Planning Association.

Introduction

This volume presents a series of quantitative indicators which are intended to illuminate some of the important aspects of the role played by scientific and R&D activities in our economic and social life not already described by existing data. A substantial number of important indicators of the state of science and research have been in existence for some time. A compendium of these and some new indicators is provided in recent publications by the National Science Board, *Science Indicators, 1974.* Most of these indicators are based on data on human and financial resources employed in research and development and on enrollments and degrees awarded in the sciences at institutions of higher learning.

The present collection contains a variety of additional indicators. In preparing them, the main emphasis was placed on developing indicators of the effects of science and research on the economy and society. Two groups of such indicators are included. One concerns the amount of economic growth which, under certain assumptions, can be attributed to industrial research. It also deals with the sequence of events between the conduct of R&D and economic growth. The other concerns the increases in life expectancy resulting from decreases in mortality rates which, based on medical opinion surveys, can be associated with certain major biomedical innovations. Development of indicators of the social or economic effects of R&D is much more difficult than development of indicators of levels of effort in science or R&D activities. Information on the economic and social effects of R&D does not exist in any ready form at present, and each such indicator requires considerable research for its own sake.

In addition to work on the economic and social effects of R&D, a number of indicators were developed concerning the level of effort in scientific and R&D activities and trends in science education which, in the view of the authors, would add to the knowledge of these subjects.

While the task of the present work is measurement, not historical analysis or testing of a particular hypothesis about the general condition of science, one substantive observation is unavoidable. Like many of the indicators already known, most of the time series in this collection have been declining from a peak point reached in the late 1960s, strongly suggesting a pervasive downturn in the state of science as measured by these different quantitative indicators.

The present report contains the results of work of a number of researchers, including Edwin Mansfield, Neil McMullen, Rory Paredes, Edward Rhodes, Joseph Schachter, Ivars Zageris, and myself. The report consists of four parts.

Part I contains a chartbook summary of the entire report. The chartbook format was chosen to make the overall results accessible to a wider audience by avoiding the detailed statistical explanations often of interest primarily to the experts in the field. The rationale, methods and sources used in developing particular indicators are described in detail in the individual chapters in Parts II to IV.

Part II includes chapters describing the development of three types of indicators dealing with the levels of R&D activities. Derived from generally known data on R&D employment and expenditures and from surveys of scientists, these indicators attempt to measure systematically certain trends in scientific and research activity not measured before.

One group of indicators attempts to develop from fragmentary information a time series describing *the level of basic scientific effort* by means of man-years worked in basic research by all scientists and engineers and also by doctoral scientists and engineers alone. Another group of indicators attempts to cumulate the annual levels of R&D activity into estimates of *the capital stock of R&D.* The third group of indicators deals with *the regional trends in the location of R&D* activities in the United States.

In Chapter 2, Ms. Paredes undertakes to measure trends in the level of scientific activity in the United States by means of two time series: (1) the number of man-years worked by all scientists and engineers in basic research, and (2) the number of doctoral scientists and engineers engaged in basic research. The results obtained with these two indicators are consistent and both show considerable growth in the level of scientific activity in the United States during the 1950s and 1960s, followed by a leveling off in the late 1960s and a subsequent decline.

In analyzing the trends in scientific and technological activities, it is important to make a distinction between basic science and technological applications. Basic research activities correspond most closely to scientific activities, while applied research and development can be more accurately considered as forms of technological investments directed toward specific fields of application. Making this distinction statistically is difficult. Nevertheless, distinctions were made in some expenditure and manpower statistics between basic research, applied research and development.

The two series developed in the chapter are complementary. The overall number of scientists and engineers in basic research is derived from the proportions of basic research expenditure to total outlay for R&D in each of the four performing sectors separately. The series of doctoral scientists and engineers is a direct estimate, derived from earlier surveys of the National Science Foundation made for the roster of scientific professional personnel and from more recent surveys of the National Academy of Sciences.

The number of man-years worked by professional scientists and engineers is chosen in preference to expenditure because the price data for deflating the expenditures is not available. There is also a real question as to whether the scientific productivity of other inputs included in the cost data is better approximated by assuming that it is in the same proportion to the productivity of scientists and engineers as their cost or that it is zero. The present indicators are based on the assumption that it is zero. These indicators are selective; they are not meant to be exclusive but a time series to complement other data.

In Chapter 3, Messrs. McMullen and Zageris undertake a sensitivity analysis by calculating R&D capital stock and measuring its growth and the ratio of net to gross R&D investment under different assumptions about the depreciation rate of R&D capital.

The economic, technological and social effects of R&D activities are generally recognized as continuing over long periods of time. The conceptual formulations of the economic effects of R&D are more developed than those of other effects, but the importance of time is the same in other fields.

Underlying any concept of the economic effects of R&D activities on productivity and economic growth is an implicit concept of R&D as a capital stock. Existing statistical information on R&D, however, consists mostly of data on the annual levels of R&D activity, measured variously by expenditure and by man-years worked. These data thus correspond to the concept of annual additions to R&D capital. This statistical limitation is inevitable because we do not know how to compound annual R&D activity data, i.e., gross investments, into a capital stock since neither the durability of R&D nor the depreciation rate of R&D investments is known. Without knowing the depreciation rate, R&D capital cannot be measured.

The question of the depreciation rate of R&D capital is vital, since the first decision that must be made in considering economic or other implications of changes in the annual levels of R&D activities is whether the R&D results are imperishable or whether their value deteriorates with time. This is precisely the question of whether the depreciation rate for R&D is zero or positive. It can be argued plausibly that R&D does indeed depreciate, at least at some positive rate. If so, a more difficult question arises—at what rate does R&D depreciate? To answer that question, however, little evidence exists.

Building on the assumptions, results and reasoning of earlier investigators, the authors explore implications of various depreciation rates ranging from zero to 20 percent per annum for total national R&D man-years and from 5 percent to 20 percent for private expenditures on industrial R&D.

Some of the results are startling. For example, even the comparatively low depreciation rate of 5 percent leads to a conclusion that almost 60 percent of present R&D investment constitutes replacement investment, i.e., that depreciation currently amounts to 60 percent of the annual R&D investment and that only 40 percent of the current R&D work contributes new capital.

In Chapter 4, Mr. Zageris analyzes R&D data for trends in the distribution of research and development activities among the nine major regions ("Census regions") of the nation. Systematic information on the geographic distribution of research and development activities in the United States has been available only since the early 1960s. These detailed data, collected by the National Science Foundation, permit analysis of location of R&D activities separately for the three major performing sectors—industry, government and academic institutions—and by their source of financing, whether government or private.

On the whole, the results show that little change occurred in the regional patterns in the location of R&D activities over the 10-year period. After adjustment for inflation, there has also been virtually no growth in the amounts of R&D activities. With respect to population, R&D activities remain relatively concentrated in the Northeast and on the West Coast, due largely to the allocation patterns of governmental expenditures. Privately financed industrial R&D, on the other hand, has been localized in the Midwest and the Middle Atlantic Regions as well as in New England.

Part III presents the results of original research conducted to develop indicators measuring growth components in the gross national product and in the national average life expectancy, which, under a set of specific assumptions, may be attributed to research and development activities. This research involves, in the economic field, analysis of *productivity growth differentials* in R&D intensive industries. Because the *diffusion of innovations* in economic, and in other, spheres is the mechanism which translates the scientific or technological discoveries into economic or social changes, case analyses are undertaken for a number of significant industrial innovations. In the health field, this research involves identification of major *life-saving discoveries* of biomedical science and assessment of their effects on the mortality rates from specific causes of death.

In Chapter 5, Professor Mansfield presents data concerning the rate of diffusion in the United States of eight major industrial innovations: numerically controlled machine tools, the basic oxygen process in steelmaking, catalytic cracking of petroleum, large-scale ammonia plants, acrylonitrile from propylene, the oxychlorination process for vinyl chloride, discrete semiconductors, and nuclear power. The extent of the savings from each of these innovations is also discussed. The results are intended to develop quantitative information on the current and recent rates of diffusion of selected industrial innovations which have had appreciable effects on productivity. The rate of diffusion of new technology is of great importance, since new techniques can have little or no impact on productivity and living standards unless they are applied and their application spreads throughout the economy.

Chapter 6 contains an analysis, by the editor, leading to an estimation of the value of economic growth (annually in constant dollars) which, within a framework of an econometric model, is attributed to business expenditures for industrial R&D. This estimate is calculated by a formula embodying the direct effects of R&D in industries performing the R&D as well as the indirect effects in the customer industries purchasing materials and equipment from the industries performing the R&D. Another set of magnitudes of the direct and the indirect effects is calculated, based on results of a different study, which suggests qualitatively similar conclusions, although it provides different estimates of the size of the indirect effects. Though highly experimental in many regards, these estimates attempt to summarize quantitatively the results of economic research in this field which consistently support the existence of substantial direct and indirect effects of industrial R&D on growth in economic productivity.

In Chapter 7, Mr. Schachter estimates increases in life expectancy occurring between 1940 and 1970 as a result of specific reductions in mortality which can be related to progress in medical science. He focuses on the reductions in mortality from nine identified causes of death, including tuberculosis, pneumonia and hypertension, for which prior surveys of medical opinion and other studies provided bases for linking them to the introduction of six particular innovations resulting from specific biomedical discoveries. The six innovations identified include, among others, penicillin and organ transplantation techniques. The total increase in longevity resulting from reductions in mortality from the nine causes is 2.4 years. This constitutes approximately one-third of the total increase in life expectancy between 1940 and 1970. These estimates are not precise in that the six innovations did not uniquely determine the changes in mortality from the nine causes; other effects were also at work. On the other hand, these innovations probably affected other causes of death as well.

Estimates of the effects of biomedical discoveries on longevity provide important but necessarily incomplete indicators of the effects of biomedical science on health. They do not reflect improvements in the state of health other than reductions in mortality nor do they reflect improvements which save patients pain and discomfort even if they do not affect their state of health.

Part IV presents indicators of the learning of science in high schools based on the educational statistics of *enrollments in science courses* and on the average *test scores in science* from standardized achievement tests administered nationally in different years.

Mr. Rhodes discusses in Chapter 8 development of the indicators of the extent of learning of science by students. One indicator deals with enrollments in high school mathematics and science courses. While a number of statistical series had to be put together by adjusting for enrollments in nonpublic schools and for differences in the grades covered, it was possible to trace the numbers of students taking science courses at the secondary school level back to 1890.

The other indicator of the learning of science by high school students is based on data obtained from large-scale tests given at the end of the students' high school years. Tracing the record of the mean scores in science from two such tests covering the period from 1957/59 to 1972/73, Mr. Rhodes finds that the amount of learning of science as measured by the test scores from one series increased from 1957/58 to 1971/72, but that it declined from 1969/70 to 1972/73 as measured by another. This trend parallels those of other indicators of the state of science and R&D which typically show a pattern in which the earlier rapid growth comes to a halt or actually reverses into a decline at some point late in the 1960s.

Nestor E. Terleckyj
Washington, D.C.
February 1976

Part I

SUMMARY

1 State of Science and Research: Some New Indicators A Chartbook Summary

Nestor E. Terleckyj

Levels of Research Inputs

(1) Number of professionals in basic research
   a. Doctoral scientists and engineers, 1960-72
   b. All scientists and engineers, 1943-73
(2) R&D man-years—all sectors
(3) Business expenditure for industrial R&D
   a. Annually
   b. Estimates of capital stock

The data on the dollar and manpower resources used in scientific and research activities are rather well developed generally. These data are used to develop several new indicators which may illuminate certain trends not apparent otherwise. One indicator attempts to answer the question of *how many scientists* actually have been working in basic science. Another attempts to view *R&D as a capital stock* compounded from annual investments, taking into account the likely possibility that the results of R&D activities are to some degree perishable. Because estimates of the rate of depreciation applicable to R&D are highly speculative and spread over a wide range, only sensitivity analyses have been undertaken, calculating the R&D capital under varying assumptions about depreciation. Two *long historical time series* were constructed using partially interpolated annual data reaching back to 1921. One measures total man-years worked by all professional R&D workers in the United States. The other series is based on private industry expenditures in constant dollars for research and development. Private industry *investments* in R&D are similar to other types of capital investments and a set of estimates of *private industry R&D capital* was constructed using different depreciation rates. The concept of capital is less clearly applicable to the combined applied R&D in all sectors. Capital estimates for basic research would also be even conceptually questionable because the accumulation of the stock of basic knowledge in the sciences is an international process, and no meaningful estimates could be derived from a compounding of the domestic level of effort series alone.

The Level of Effort in American Science

Chart 1-1 depicts trends in the level of scientific activity in the United States using two time series: (1) the number of man-years worked by all scientists and engineers in basic research, estimated from detailed R&D expenditure and employment data and (2) the number of doctoral scientists and engineers engaged in basic research, derived from survey data. The results obtained with these two indicators are consistent, and both show considerable growth in the level of scientific activity in the United States during the 1950s and 1960s, a leveling off in the late '60s, and a subsequent decline.

CHART 1-1
ESTIMATED NUMBER OF SCIENTISTS AND ENGINEERS
AND OF DOCTORAL SCIENTISTS AND ENGINEERS
ENGAGED IN BASIC RESEARCH, U.S. TOTAL,
SELECTED YEARS, 1954-73

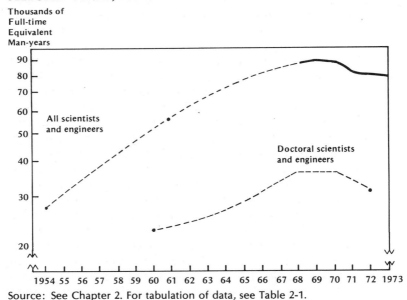

Source: See Chapter 2. For tabulation of data, see Table 2-1.

4

Man-years of Scientists and Engineers in R&D, 1921-74

Chart 1-2 provides estimates of research and development activity measured in man-years worked by R&D scientists and engineers for the period from 1921 to 1973. Such data are sometimes taken as a proxy for an output measure which is not available for R&D. It is a valid concept in this role but only to the extent that the assumption equating input and output can be accepted. Then such an indicator may be interpreted to represent the quantity of *new* research knowledge produced during each year of the period. It does not describe the stock of knowledge.

CHART 1-2
ESTIMATED MAN-YEARS OF SCIENTISTS AND ENGINEERS
ENGAGED IN RESEARCH AND DEVELOPMENT
IN THE UNITED STATES, 1921-74

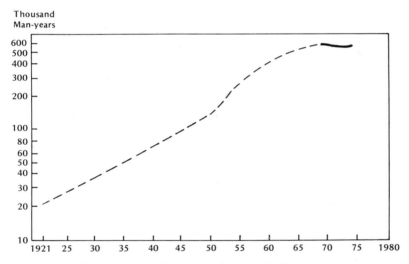

Source: See Chapter 3. For tabulation of data, see Table 3-1.

Business Investment in R&D, 1921-74

The series in Chart 1-3 represents an attempt to obtain an approximate long-term estimate of the constant dollar investment by private business in industrial R&D. The data in current dollars for the years 1953-74 have been reported by the National Science Foundation. Estimates of the cost of industrial R&D

performance for selected years from 1921 to 1953 were made in an earlier study by the author. These estimates were adjusted to exclude government financed industrial R&D for the years 1940-51, and the resulting series was linked to the NSF data. The entire series was then converted to 1973 dollars by means of the GNP price deflator.

CHART 1-3
ESTIMATED CONSTANT DOLLAR ANNUAL EXPENDITURE
BY PRIVATE INDUSTRY FOR PERFORMANCE OF
RESEARCH AND DEVELOPMENT, UNITED STATES, 1921-74

Billions of
1973 Dollars

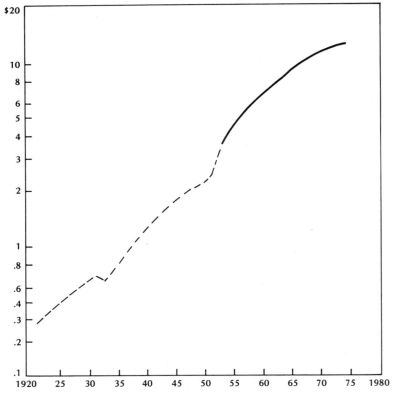

Source: See Chapter 3. For tabulation of data, see Table 3-5.

Underlying the concept of productive effects of R&D activities is an implicit concept of R&D as a capital stock. The existing statistical information on R&D, however, is primarily oriented toward the annual levels of R&D activity, and thus corresponds to the concept of annual flows of investment in R&D. Estimation of R&D capital as part of official statistics is not practical because we do not know how to compound annual R&D investments into capital stock. Therefore, the only inferences that can be made about the growth of the store of R&D capital have to rely on sensitivity analyses which map out the implication of alternative assumptions about the depreciation rate for R&D, varying it over its entire plausible range.

While basic conceptual difficulties may arise regarding the concept of capital stock for all R&D activities, which include such components as basic scientific research or government financed R&D, these difficulties are not so critical in the case of business outlays for R&D. Private expenditures for industrial R&D have many of the same characteristics as other capital investments by industry. They follow the fluctuations in the corporate cash flow (retained earnings and depreciation), their expenditures and returns are spread over time, and their rates of returns vary widely. Chart 1-4 shows the constant dollar business expenditures for R&D from the previous chart cumulated into capital stock, assuming a three-year lag between expenditure and its embodiment in capital and a straight line depreciation thereafter calculated at the different rates shown. So measured, the R&D capital stock grew between the years 1968 and 1976 (which, because of the three-year lag, reflects the data through 1965 and 1973, respectively) at an annual rate of 6.8, 6.3, 5.9, and 5.5 percent, respectively, for the assumed depreciation rates of 5, 10, 15, and 20 percent.

Selected Economic and Social Effects of Science and Research

   (1) Economic growth effects
      a. Value of economic growth attributed to industrial R&D
      b. Rate of economic growth attributable to R&D
      c. R&D intensity of the economy

CHART 1-4
CAPITAL STOCK OF PRIVATELY FINANCED R&D
EXPENDITURES FOR PERFORMANCE OF INDUSTRIAL
RESEARCH AND DEVELOPMENT
CUMULATED BY ASSUMING A THREE-YEAR LAG AND
DIFFERENT STRAIGHT LINE DEPRECIATION RATES, UNITED
STATES

Billions of
1973 Dollars

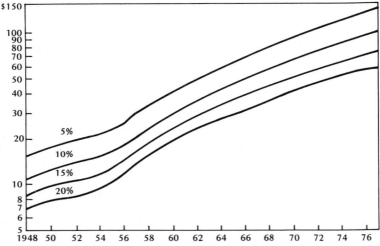

Source: See Chapter 3. For tabulation of data, see Table 3-6.

(2) Diffusion of industrial innovations
   a. Diffusion of new producers' goods
   b. Changes in the productive capacity

In attempting to identify the effects of science on social or economic conditions, it is not practical to separate the effects of basic science or basic research from the effects of applied research or of development work. The reason is simply that all these effects are joint. In order for any social or economic change to occur, the complete chain of work from basic scientific discoveries to their practical implementations, i.e., embodiment in an actual innovation, has to be completed before even the first application can occur. From then on, the amount of change cumulated up to a given time depends on the extent of the diffusion of the given innovation which has been achieved by then. Even though the actual relationships between basic discov-

8

eries and operational innovations are not simply one-to-one, in exploring the effects of science on society it is necessary to *focus on innovations*. Innovations are the observable means by which scientific discoveries are translated into social and economic change. The *indicator of the economic effects of R&D* shown here is derived from an econometric model in which the results of R&D are implicitly embodied in innovations in products and production processes without an explicit identification of particular innovations. *Actual case histories of diffusion* of industrial innovations are charted here by means of the percentage indicators of the penetration of new producers' goods into their respective markets and of the changes in the productive capacity which follow, with various time lags, the introduction of new equipment or systems. The *indicator of the effects of biomedical research on life expectancy* is derived directly from the estimates of the effects of six specific innovations on the mortality rates from nine causes of death. Diffusion of these innovations through the health practice systems and its correlation with the reduction of the respective death rates remain to be explored.

Value of Economic Growth Attributable to Industrial R&D

The indicator of the effects of R&D on economic growth, shown in Chart 1-5, is derived from the results of a number of statistical and econometric studies of the link between industrial R&D and the growth of productivity, and hence of economic growth. These studies have established (not necessarily definitively but reflecting the present state of knowledge on the subject) that the privately financed industrial R&D apparently contributes to economic growth through a positive effect on productivity growth and that, in addition to the effects of R&D on the productivity of industries in which it is performed, there are evidently also indirect effects on the productivity of customer industries which purchase their intermediate and capital goods from the R&D-intensive industries.

While these conclusions are reasonably well established qualitatively, the particular nature of the relationships involved and the magnitude of the effects are subject to more uncertainty. Quantitative estimates have been made, however. Chart 1-5 traces the value of economic growth calculated from a formula discussed further in Chart 1-6 (see next section), which is based on the estimate of the productivity effects of R&D. While different

CHART 1-5
VALUE OF ECONOMIC GROWTH ATTRIBUTED TO PRODUC-
TIVITY EFFECTS OF INDUSTRIAL R&D. TWO SETS OF ESTIMATES
OF DIRECT AND INDIRECT PRODUCTIVITY EFFECTS ON
GROSS BUSINESS PRODUCT, 1953-73 (in 1973 dollars).

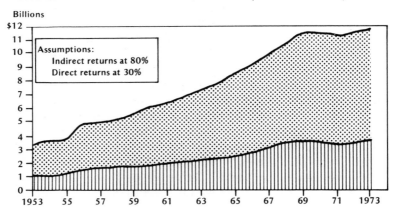

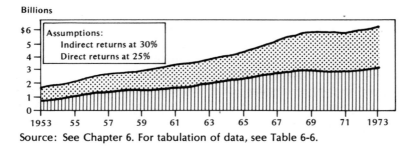

Source: See Chapter 6. For tabulation of data, see Table 6-6.

studies in this field led to similar estimates of the direct return to
R&D, there are some differences in the estimates of the indirect
returns, though studies using different methods suggest that
such returns apparently exist and that they are high. Accordingly,
Chart 1-5 shows two sets of the economic growth effects calculated with assumptions obtained from two independent studies
cited in the sources.

Chart 1-5 shows the format in which the economic effects of R&D
can be measured. The estimates themselves should be considered highly tentative. Much additional research must be done

to establish, among other things, the actual timing of the impact or the stability of the calculated effects from year to year.

Calculating Economic Returns from R&D Investments

Chart 1-6 shows the economic returns to R&D calculated in percentage terms from the formula

$$r = dI + i(.85 \, I).$$

The formula shows, for the business sector, the percentage rate of growth in productivity (i.e., output per unit of input), r, as the sum of direct rate of productivity return, d, times the R&D intensity of the business sector, I (i.e., private business expenditure for R&D divided by the business gross product), and the indirect rate of productivity return, i, times the indirect R&D investment intensity (which differs from the direct R&D intensity by excluding the proportion, 15 percent, embodied in sales outside the business sector). The same two sets of alternative estimates of the rates of return are shown as in the preceding chart.

In calculating the growth rate, the R&D intensity ratio for the business sector (see Chart 1-7) is multiplied by the productivity rate of return to R&D for the same year. This procedure assumes that the average rates of return computed for long periods actually apply to each individual year, and that there is no time lag between R&D and its embodiment in economic growth. (The reader may wish to modify these assumptions individually.)

The percentage rate of growth is converted to dollar amounts by applying it to the business gross product in constant dollars for the given year.

R&D Intensity of the American Economy

The national investment rate in research and development, measured by privately financed R&D in relation to the volume of the private sector production, constitutes a basic indicator relevant to the analysis of productivity and economic growth. (The indicator excludes governmental defense, space and health R&D because little if any increase in *measured* economic productivity appears to result from this R&D).

11

Such an indicator of national R&D intensity, shown in Chart 1-7, records continued growth from less than 0.7 percent in the early 1950s to more than 1.2 percent in 1969, declining thereafter to 1.1 percent. The business sector gross product for which the private

CHART 1-6
ANNUAL RATE OF PRODUCTIVITY GROWTH IN THE
BUSINESS GROSS PRODUCT ATTRIBUTED TO
INDUSTRIAL R&D UNDER DIFFERENT
ASSUMPTIONS ABOUT THE MAGNITUDE OF DIRECT
AND INDIRECT RETURNS

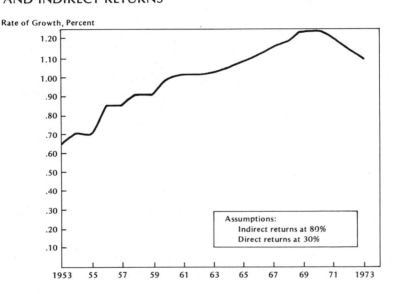

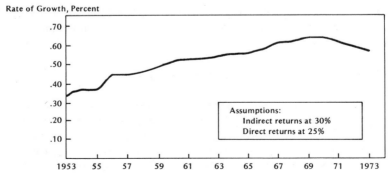

Source: See Chapter 6. For tabulation of data, see Table 6-5.

CHART 1-7
PRIVATELY FINANCED INDUSTRIAL RESEARCH AND
DEVELOPMENT AS A PERCENT OF BUSINESS GROSS
PRODUCT IN THE UNITED STATES, 1953-73

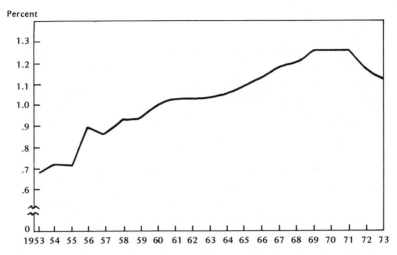

Source: See Chapter 6. For tabulation of data, see Table 6-4.

R&D intensity is charted represents 96 percent of the private economy and 84 percent of the total GNP.

Because of the lack of data, international comparisons of the industrial R&D intensity can be made only to a limited extent and in terms of a more inclusive ratio of all nondefense R&D to total GNP. The following is an array of selected industrial countries by the ratio for the year 1971:

	1971 Civilian R&D as percent of GNP
Japan	2.1%
W. Germany	2.0
U.S.	1.8
France	1.3
Canada	1.0

The ratio for the United States is about 50 percent higher than the 1971 ratio shown in the chart because it includes relatively more R&D (all nonprofit and all nondefense federal R&D) than economic activity (government purchases of goods and services).

Diffusion of New Products and Processes

The process by which industrial research and development eventually leads to growth in productivity and hence to economic growth consists of a sequence of events: conduct of R&D, development of new product and process prototypes from the successful R&D projects, the first operational application of some of these products or processes and subsequent diffusion of these innovations.

Chart 1-8 shows the rates of diffusion of some recent industrial innovations: discrete semiconductors, turbine engine aircraft (turboprops and jets) and numerically controlled machine tools. Introduction of these new products is shown as a percentage of the relevant group total. Also included is the more controversial case of nuclear electric power. (Productivity gains from that innovation have been questioned on the grounds of the net value of total social effects and sometimes even in commercial terms alone.) The four cases in Chart 1-8 relate to the diffusion of new producer goods. Analogous diffusion processes occur in the case of innovations in consumer goods, household activities, professional practices and government.

Upgrading Productive Capacity

While a new type of equipment or method of production may quickly come to dominate additions to the productive capacity, changes in the productive capacity itself, on which the productivity of the industry depends, will be completed only after the old equipment is retired and the new productive system replaces the entire capital stock.

Chart 1-9 illustrates seven specific cases of changeover of productive capacity in a variety of industries, including aviation, petroleum refining, steel, basic chemicals, plastics, synthetic fibers, and electric power. Such innovations may take a longer or shorter period of time depending on, among other things, the life span of the capital equipment. In aviation, where equipment

CHART 1-8
SHARE OF THE MARKET OF SELECTED NEW PRODUCERS'
GOODS OR RATE OF DISPLACEMENT OF AN OLDER DEVICE,*
FOUR CASES, 1952-74

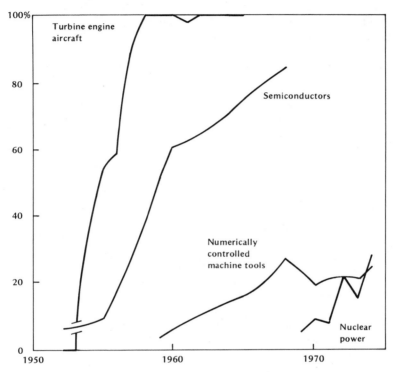

* *For aircraft:* Number of aircraft on order for delivery to U.S. scheduled airlines at year end; turbine engine aircraft as percent of all aircraft (excluding helicopters).

For semiconductors: Value of output; discrete semiconductors as percent of discrete semiconductors and receiving tubes. (After 1967, this comparison is less meaningful because of further technological changes.)

For machine tools: Value of shipments; numerically controlled machine tools as percent of all metal cutting machine tools.

For nuclear power: Increase in capacity; nuclear capacity as percent of all new capacity installed.

Source: See Chapter 5. For tabulation of data, see Appendix Table 5-2. For aircraft, see Air Transport Association of America, *Air Transport Facts and Figures for 1953-65.*

CHART 1-9

PERCENT OF PRODUCTIVE CAPACITY BASED ON THE
INNOVATION, SELECTED INNOVATIONS,
UNITED STATES, 1937-1974

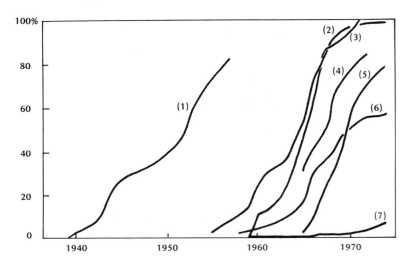

(1) Catalytic cracking capacity as percent of total U.S. petroleum cracking capacity (data discontinued after 1957).

(2) Number of turbine (turbojet and turboprop) aircraft as percent of total aircraft fleet of U.S. scheduled airlines (excludes helicopters).

(3) Percent of acrylonitrile output produced from propylene.

(4) Percent of U.S. vinyl chloride capacity that uses oxychlorination process.

(5) Capacity of large-scale ammonia plants (600 tons/day or more) as percent off U.S. total ammonia capacity.

(6) Percent of steel output produced by basic oxygen process.

(7) Nuclear capacity as percent of all installed electrical generating capacity.

Source: See Chapter 5. For tabulation of data, see Appendix Table 5-2. For aircraft, see Air Transport Association of America, *Air Transport Facts and Figures*, various years.

life is comparatively short (under 10 years for aircraft), outstanding delivery orders for engine aircraft (turboprops and jets) rose in only five years from 0 percent of all orders in 1953 to 100 percent in 1958. However, the total operating fleet still consisted of two-thirds (64 percent) piston-engine craft in 1962, and it was not until 1969, or 13 years after the first introduction of the new type of aircraft, that full conversion (95 percent) was accomplished in commercial aviation. In many other industries, equipment lives are much longer and capital conversion takes correspondingly longer. In steelmaking, oil refining and chemicals, the life of equipment may range between 10 and 20 years, and in electric utilities it typically exceeds, sometimes substantially, 20 years.

Major Life-saving Advances in Medicine since 1940

Table 1-1 identifies six major medical advances and the nine disease categories in which they have effected reductions in mortality. The table attributes changes in the life expectancy resulting from the reductions in mortality in these categories to these innovations in an attempt to obtain a quantitative judgment about the possible magnitude of their life-saving effects. These innovations were identified from surveys of the opinions of medical practitioners and medical researchers. The calculations were based on mortality data by causes of death and on estimates of the life expectancy lost. Certain observations are suggested by the data in the table: (1) there appear to exist important preventive elements in the nine applications of these innovations; (2) of the six innovations, three were introduced in the 1940s, two in the 1950s and one in the 1960s. This pattern may reflect the existence of time lags between the introduction of innovations and the time their impact becomes apparent and recognized by medical opinion or in the data; and (3) four of the six innovations are embodied in pharmaceutical or serological products, one represents a diagnostic procedure and one a surgical procedure.

Mortality Rates from Nine Specified Causes

Chart 1-10 shows the trends in the mortality rates from nine specific causes of death. The reduction in these rates has been associated with six specific major medical innovations introduced after 1940 and a chain of other advances. These advances

Table 1-1

MEDICAL ADVANCES AND LIFE EXPECTANCY, UNITED STATES, 1940-70

Disease Category and Classification Code (ICDA 8th Revision Codes)	Important Medical Advance	Approximate Time of Introduction	Other Relevant Medical Advances	Death Rates* per 100,000 Population		Estimate of Increased Life Expectancy at Birth (Years)*
				In Year Prior to Medical Advance Listed in Column (2)	In 1970	
(1)	(2)	(3)	(4)	(5)	(6)	(7)
Tuberculosis (010-019)	Streptomycin	1944	Isoniazid, para-amino salicylic acid, rifampin, ethambutol	38.8	2.6	.80
Poliomyelitis (040-044)	Salk vaccine	1955	Sabin vaccine	1.0	0.1	.03
Syphilis (090-097)	Penicillin	1943	Penicillin G procaine and G benzathine, tetracycline, erythromycin	2.9	0.2	.05
Cancer of the uterus (180-182)	Pap smear	1943	Radiological therapy, surgery, chemotherapy	11.6	5.9	.15
Rheumatic fever and rheumatic heart disease (390-398)	Penicillin	1943	Open heart surgery	21.9	7.3	.32
Hypertension and hypertensive heart disease (400-404)	Hydralazine	1950	Reserpine, thiazides, guanethidine, propranolol, methyldopa	30.7	11.4	.33
Pneumonia (480-486)	Penicillin	1943	Vaccines against influenza and pneumonia, tetramycin, erythromycin	40.3	29.0	.53
Appendicitis (540-543)	Penicillin	1943	Tetracycline, improved blood typing and storage, surgical and anesthesiologic progress	5.4	0.7	.12
Chronic nephritis, renal sclerosis and chronic pyelonephritis (582-584, 590)	Organ transplantation technology	1962	Dialysis, immunosuppressive therapy, histological matching, organ preservation, antibiotics	10.2	7.7	.05

*Rates for years prior to 1970 adjusted to 1970 basis to allow for revisions in coding rules and in decennial revisions of international classification of diseases. There is a difference in the estimate of increased life expectancy between the sum of the individual entries (2.38) and the estimate for the nine causes combined (2.32) which is due to interaction effects.

and the causes of death they affected were listed in Table 1-1. Data in Chart 1-10 are shown without adjustment for the decennial revisions of the international classification of diseases. This is indicated by the breaks in the time series. The estimates presented in Table 1-1 were made on a consistent (adjusted) basis.

It should be noted that the attribution of declines in mortality to medical advances is based on expert opinion rather than on scientific observation. Precise estimates of changes in mortality attributable to particular medical advances would require identification of all the other effects on the specified causes of death which were present during the period, as well as of the effects of these innovations on all the causes of death not included in these estimates.

Learning of Science in High Schools

 (1) Test scores in science of 17-year-olds
 (2) Enrollments in science courses in high schools
 (3) Enrollments in mathematics and science courses as percent of total enrollments

The information on enrollments and degrees awarded in science is quite well developed at the higher education level. Here, several indicators are provided which describe the study of *science in high schools*. Data on science in high schools may foreshadow future developments at the higher education level. It may also forecast changes in the level of general scientific comprehension of the population at large, because for most adults their only formal education in sciences will remain whatever science courses they had in high school.

Three indicators are provided. One attempts to measure trends in the level of knowledge of science by 17-year-olds. It is obtained by linking mean scores from two series of *tests* given a number of times in various years, starting in 1957. Another indicator shows the ratio of high school *enrollments* in mathematics and science courses to all high school enrollments for the period since 1948 covering grades 7 through 12. The third series offers the *long historical view* of the transition from an era in the 1890s, when only a small proportion of the population had any high school education, including science courses, to an era when

CHART 1-10

DEATH RATES FOR SPECIFIED CAUSES OF DEATH, UNITED STATES, 1940-73 (rates are per 100,000 population)

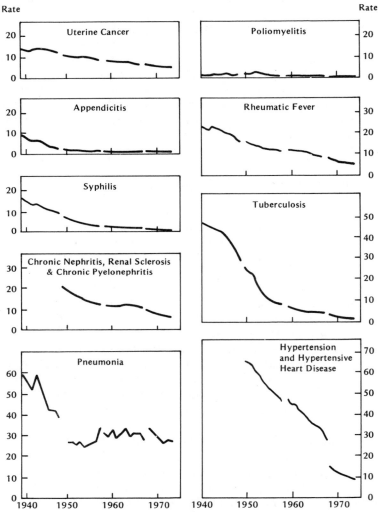

Note: Data not adjusted for revisions in international classification of diseases effective in 1949, 1958 and 1968.

Source: See Chapter 7. For tabulation of data, see Table 7-3.

high school attendance became nearly a common experience and science course enrollments increased even more.

Knowledge of Science by 17-Year-Olds

One indicator of the state of science in society is the extent of knowledge of science by the youth. Chart 1-11 shows an indicator of the learning of science by high school students at the end of their high school years based on the data obtained from large-scale tests, tracing the record of the mean scores in science from two such tests covering the period from 1957-58 to 1972-73. The amount of learning of science as measured by the test scores from one series increased from 1957-58 to 1971-72, but declined from 1967-70 to 1972-73 as measured by another test. It should be noted that the tests in the earlier series were taken by samples of high school students while the tests in the later series reflected a sampling of the entire population of 17-year-olds.

The reader should be aware that these results, while quite provocative, are highly experimental. We have very little experience in interpreting the test score information. Although the present results cannot be ignored, they should be viewed with caution. Also, in the case of science test scores, unlike most physical and economic measurements, both the object being measured and the measuring rod are not constant. Many important discoveries were made in science during the period covered by the indicator. The tests have been changed to reflect the new knowledge, but also possibly in other ways. Yet there is no reason to think that changes in the tests would bias downward the result for the latest year, and viewed together with the information in the next two charts, these results do not appear improbable.

Enrollments in Science Courses Relative to Total High School Enrollments

Enrollment in mathematics and science courses in high school, as given by the data for selected survey years, grew relative to total high school enrollments for a long period, from 1948 to 1970, and then declined. The decline was sharper for mathematics, where the percentage ratio dropped 5 points (from 76 to 71 percent), than for science, where it declined 2 points (from 69 to 67 percent). This decline returned the ratio for mathematics to its level of the 1950s and the ratio for the science course enrollments

CHART 1-11

MEAN SCORES IN THE IOWA TEST OF EDUCATION AND
DEVELOPMENT (ITED) AND THE NATIONAL ASSESSMENT OF
EDUCATIONAL PROGRESS (NAEP) PERCENTAGE CORRECT
FOR 17-YEAR-OLDS

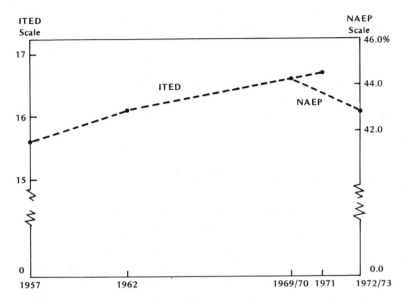

Note: Scales have been aligned so that the NAEP score for 1969-70 corresponds
to the interpolated value of the ITED score for the same year.

Source: See Chapter 8. For tabulation of data, see Table 8-4.

to the level of the early 1960s. The practices of curriculum design
were sufficiently stable to rule out a sudden change in the course
design. Therefore, the proportion of enrollments in these
courses relative to total enrollments can be taken as indicative of
the percentage of students taking mathematics or science
courses.

CHART 1-12

HIGH SCHOOL ENROLLMENTS IN MATHEMATICS AND SCIENCE COURSES AS PERCENT OF TOTAL HIGH SCHOOL ENROLLMENTS, GRADES 7-12, U.S. PUBLIC SCHOOLS, SELECTED SCHOOL YEARS, 1948/9-1972/3

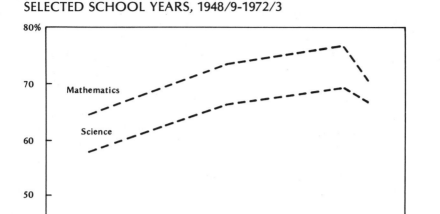

Source: See Chapter 8. For tabulation of data, see Table 8-1.

Enrollments in High School Science Courses

Chart 1-13 shows the total population of high school age, high school enrollments and enrollments in high school science courses since 1890 (grades 9-12 through 1965; grades 7-12 for 1949-73). These long-term trends place the recent changes in historical perspective. There was a tremendous growth in the absolute numbers of high school enrollments and enrollments in science courses during the period. Over the long period, the proportion of the population attending high school grew from less than 20 percent to over 90 percent. Enrollments in high school science courses grew more or less rapidly than all high school enrollments at various times, but over the whole period they increased more than total high school enrollments.

Rapid growth in science enrollments ended after 1970, when they declined absolutely as well as relatively to high school enrollments, as was shown in the preceding chart.

23

CHART 1-13
HIGH SCHOOL AGE POPULATION, SCHOOL ENROLLMENT AND SCIENCE COURSE ENROLLMENT, 1890-1974

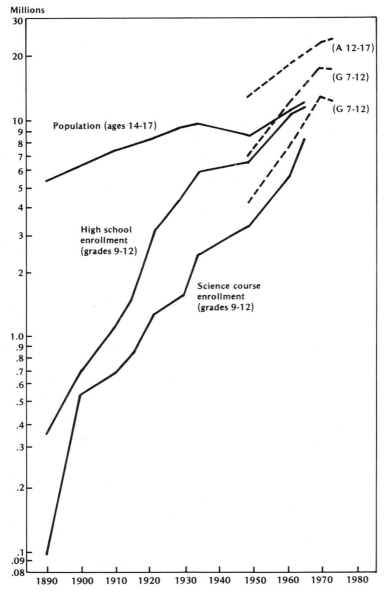

Source: See Chapter 8. For tabulation of data, see Tables 8-1 and 8-2.

Regional Distribution of Research and Development

(1) Geography of national R&D expenditure, total and per capita amounts, 1973
(2) Regional trends in R&D performance, 1964-73
    a. By source of financing
    b. By performing sector
(3) Regional patterns in industrial and academic R&D manpower
    a. R&D scientists and engineers in industry, 1966
    b. Teaching and R&D in colleges and universities, 1973

Interest in the *geographic dimensions* of research and development was originally stimulated by policymakers concerned with the allocation of federal R&D funds among the regions. With the data accumulated over the past decade, it is now possible to obtain some general indicators not only of *government* spending for R&D but the spatial dimension of *industrial*, governmental and *academic R&D* in the United States in general. The graphs that follow show for the nine major regions ("census regions") of the United States the total and per capita amounts of R&D expenditure (excluding for lack of data the relatively small amounts of expenditure for R&D performed by nonprofit institutions other than academic). Because the geography of research and development appears to be interesting primarily in its relation to the distribution of population, after the main absolute dimensions have been portrayed, most graphs show the regional data on a per capita basis. (Other meaningful comparisons, not made here, could relate the regional distribution of R&D to the distribution of industrial or academic activites.) The regional trends in the *constant dollar cost* of R&D performance are examined in detail by the source of financing of R&D and by the performing sector. Selected regional patterns regarding the distribution of R&D manpower in industry and academic institutions are also included.

Geography of R&D in the United States

The two maps in Chart 1-14 show the distribution among the nine regions of the nation of the total cost of research and development of the federal government, industry and colleges and universities combined. (This constitutes the national total except for the comparatively small amounts spent for R&D conducted in

CHART 1-14
TOTAL AND PER CAPITA EXPENDITURE FOR R&D
PERFORMANCE BY THE FEDERAL GOVERNMENT,
INDUSTRY AND COLLEGES AND UNIVERSITIES BY CENSUS
REGION, 1973

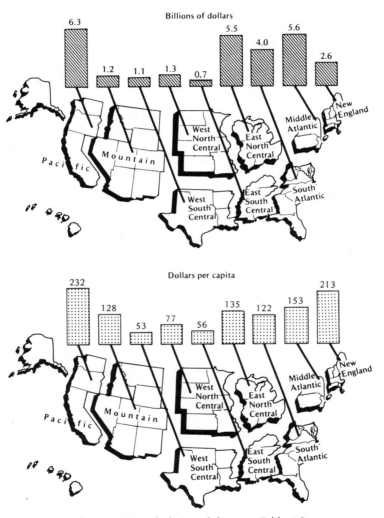

Source: See Chapter 4. For tabulation of data, see Table 4-2.

nonacademic nonprofit institutions and by the state governments outside state universities.) The map at the top shows how

the total of $28.2 billion spent for the conduct of R&D in 1973 was distributed, in absolute amounts, among the nine regions. The map shows the largest expenditure in the Pacific region and also large amounts, over $4 billion, in the Middle Atlantic, East North Central and South Atlantic regions.

Analytically, the extent of regional specialization in R&D and the degree of geographical dispersion of the R&D activities can be more clearly perceived when portrayed relative to the distribution of population, e.g., on a per capita basis, rather than in absolute amounts.

The amounts spent for R&D per capita in the nine regions charted in the lower map show a different geographical picture. First, because to some degree the distribution of R&D in the United States correlates with the distribution of population among regions, the range of variation among regions is reduced. Also, the relative preeminence of the New England states becomes apparent. These states and the Pacific region show the highest per capita expenditure while the East South Central and the West South Central regions show the lowest.

Trends in the Geography of American R&D, 1964-73

The geographical data for R&D is available for only the comparatively short period since the early 1960s. According to this information, there has been on the whole very little change in the per capita expenditure for R&D in the individual regions as well as in the United States as a whole, after deflating the R&D expenditure by the GNP price deflator. (A more specific index for the total R&D expenditure is not available.) As can be seen from Chart 1-15, the largest changes were a decline in the Pacific region (occurring between 1967 and 1970) and an increase in per capita R&D expenditures in New England (from 1964 to 1967). There was also a considerable percentage decline in the West South Central region. Other changes in either direction were small.

27

CHART 1-15

REGIONAL TRENDS IN PER CAPITA EXPENDITURE FOR R&D
PERFORMANCE, 1964-73 (in 1973 dollars)

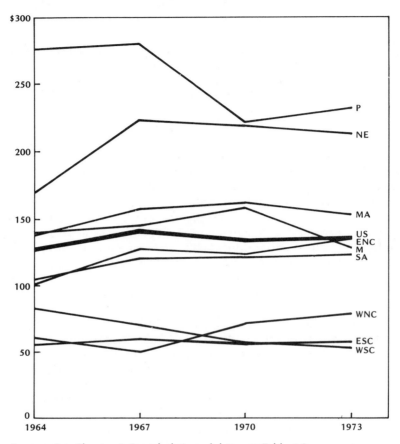

Source: See Chapter 4. For tabulation of data, see Table 4-3.

*Regional Trends in Governmental and Private R&D
Spending*

As can be seen from Chart 1-16, regional patterns for federal and
nonfederal (mostly industry) R&D expenditures have been rather stable. Government expenditure patterns changed more than
those of private expenditure. Declines in government spending
for R&D account for all of the decline in the total expenditures in
the Pacific and West South Central regions. The real private per

CHART 1-16

REGIONAL TRENDS IN PER CAPITA EXPENDITURE FOR R&D
PERFORMANCE BY SOURCE OF FINANCING, 1964-73 (in 1973
dollars)

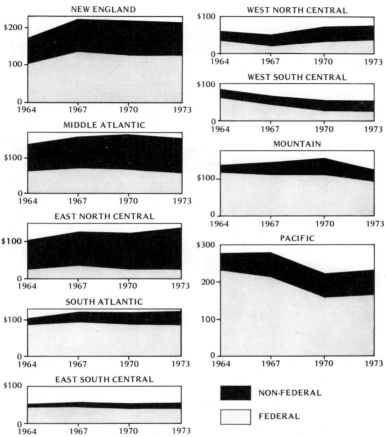

Source: See Chapter 4. For tabulation of data, see Table 4-3.

capita expenditure increased in each of the nine regions while
the federal expenditure declined in three and grew in one region
between 1964 and 1973, ignoring smaller changes in either
direction. The largest absolute growth in the real private expenditure for R&D occurred in the East North Central region (Ohio,
Michigan, Indiana, Illinois, and Wisconsin). The largest federal
increase occurred in New England.

CHART 1-17

REGIONAL TRENDS IN PER CAPITA EXPENDITURE FOR R&D
PERFORMANCE BY PERFORMING SECTOR, 1964-73 (in 1973
dollars)

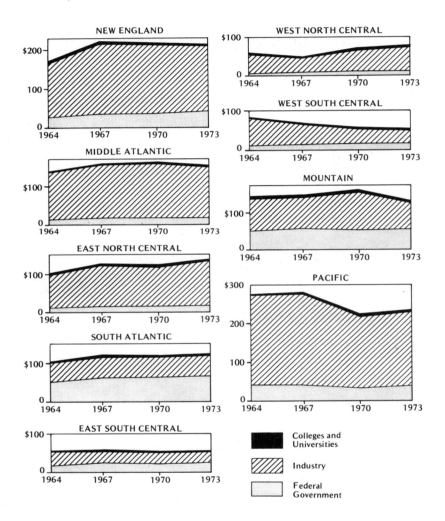

Sources: See Chapter 4. For tabulation of data, see Table 4-4.

Geography of R&D Performance by Sector

The nine panels in Chart 1-17 show that industrial performance dominates R&D in most regions, with the exception of the South Atlantic, which includes the substantial federal R&D establishment in the Maryland-Virginia-Washington, D.C., area. The industrial R&D performance includes all the private industry expenditure for R&D as well as the federally financed R&D work performed in industry. Growth in the R&D performed in the East North Central region reflects growth of the R&D performed in industry, and the declines in the R&D in the Pacific and the West South Central regions represent declines in industrial R&D. On the other hand, the slight growth in the South Atlantic region's R&D resulted from the growth in federally performed R&D.

Regional Distribution of Industrial R&D

The data on regional distribution of industrial R&D employment are available only for selected years, with the latest complete data available for 1966. Chart 1-18 shows the regional distribution of scientists and engineers employed in industrial R&D, relative to the distribution of the labor force. It shows the highest numbers in the New England and Pacific regions and the lowest in the Southern and Mountain regions.

Geography of Research and of Teaching by Academic Scientists and Engineers

Scientists and engineers employed in the academic sector are rather evenly distributed relative to population. As can be seen from the middle graph in Chart 1-19, the highest per capita concentration of academic scientists and engineers (in New England) is not quite twice as large as in the region with their lowest concentration (East South Central states).

The proportion of time academic scientists and engineers allocate to teaching is also rather stable among the regions, varying from 70 to 81 percent. The proportion of their time spent in R&D activities varies from 13 to 24 percent, with the lowest and the highest percentages occurring in the East South Central and New England states, respectively.

CHART 1-18
NUMBER OF SCIENTISTS AND ENGINEERS IN INDUSTRIAL RESEARCH AND DEVELOPMENT PER 10,000 WORKERS IN THE LABOR FORCE, 1966

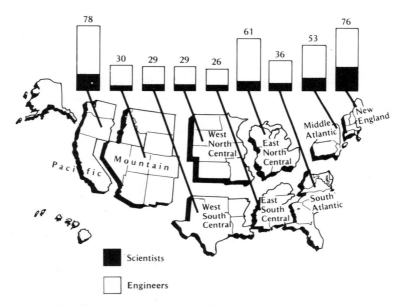

Source: See Chapter 4. For tabulation of data, see Table 4-5.

CHART 1-19
FULL-TIME EQUIVALENT SCIENTISTS AND ENGINEERS EMPLOYED IN COLLEGES AND UNIVERSITIES IN TEACHING, R&D AND OTHER ACTIVITIES, BY CENSUS REGION, 1974

Number in Thousands

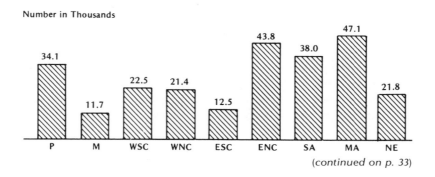

(continued on p. 33)

CHART 1-19 (*continued*)

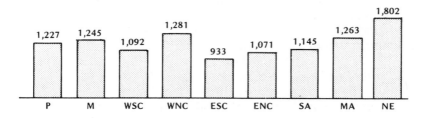

Percentage Distribution of Time by Activity

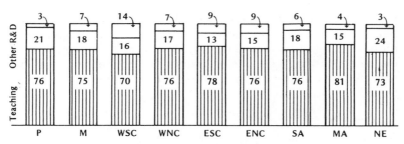

Source: See Chapter 4. For tabulation of data, see Table 4-6.

Indicators for Selected Sectors of the Economy and Society

(1) Civilian labor force
   Scientists and engineers as a percent of the labor force
(2) Agriculture
   Productivity of land
(3) Industry
   R&D and the productivity growth of industries
(4) Periodicals
   Circulation of general interest scientific periodicals

This section contains *miscellaneous indicators* which do not fit into the other sections. One indicator is the ratio of all scientists and engineers and of R&D scientists and engineers to the total *labor force*. Another is the rate of *productivity growth for groups of industries* categorized on the basis of differences in their levels of R&D intensity, with the R&D intensity defined in a new way to include not only direct industry R&D expenditure but also the

R&D "content" of goods purchased by an industry from other industries. Also included are time series on the productivity of land, i.e., *yields per acre* for principal crops, and trends in the *circulation of periodicals* with substantial scientific content but aimed at a general audience.

Scientists and Engineers as a Percent of the Labor Force

One indicator of the technological development of an economy is the proportion of technological professionals in the labor force. Chart 1-20 shows such a basic indicator of the technological and scientific intensity of the labor force. The ratio grew from less than 1.0 percent in 1950 to nearly 1.9 percent in 1968-70, and then declined to 1.7 percent in 1973. This decline does not necessarily represent attrition of trained persons through retirement or death. Changes of career, for example, from engineering to accounting of a person trained in engineering, may be reflected as declines in the number of engineers in the labor force.

CHART 1-20
ALL SCIENTISTS AND ENGINEERS AND R&D SCIENTISTS AND ENGINEERS AS A PERCENT OF TOTAL CIVILIAN LABOR FORCE IN THE UNITED STATES, 1950-73

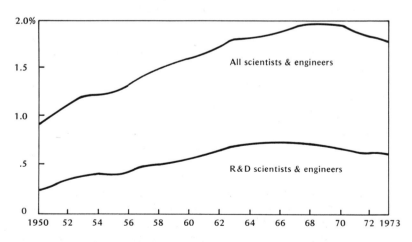

Source: For tabulation of data, see Table 1-2.

Table 1-2

ALL SCIENTISTS AND ENGINEERS
AND R&D SCIENTISTS AND ENGINEERS
AS A PERCENT OF TOTAL CIVILIAN LABOR FORCE
IN THE UNITED STATES, 1950-73

Year	All Scientists and Engineers	R&D Scientists and Engineers
1950	.89%	.25%
1951	.99	.28
1952	1.10	.33
1953	1.19	.36
1954	1.23	.38
1955	1.25	.38
1956	1.31	.41
1957	1.43	.46
1958	1.48	.49
1959	1.55	.53
1960	1.58	.55
1961	1.63	.58
1962	1.71	.62
1963	1.78	.66
1964	1.82	.68
1965	1.84	.69
1966	1.87	.69
1967	1.91	.72
1968	1.94	.70
1969	1.94	.68
1970	1.93	.65
1971	1.86	.63
1972	1.78	.61
1973	1.76	.60

SOURCES

Labor force data: Executive Office of the President, Council of Economic Advisers, Economic Report of the President, 1974 (Washington, D.C.: U.S. Government Printing Office, 1974); Scientists and engineers data: for the years 1950-70, U.S. Department of Labor, Bureau of Labor Statistics, Employment of Scientists and Engineers, 1950-70, Bulletin 1781 (Washington, D.C., 1973); for the years 1971-73, National Science Foundation, National Patterns of R&D Resources, Funds and Manpower in the United States, 1953-74, NSF 74-304 (Washington, D.C.: U.S. Government Printing Office, 1974).

The second curve shows the scientific and technological manpower engaged in R&D, i.e., in the identifiable inventive and innovative activities, as a percent of the labor force. Its movement follows that of the first indicator but at a lower level.

Productivity of Land

A basic indicator of productivity in agriculture is productivity of land. While technology, capital and agricultural labor are variables, agricultural land is fixed, at least within relatively narrow limits. The United States has a long history of continued agricultural research which evidently has built up a substantial store of knowledge capital since its inception in 1861.

The individual panels in Chart 1-21 show output per acre of harvested land for major crops. The chart shows, in addition to large annual variations, evidence of a possible long-term slowdown in the yields, especially for cotton and soybeans.

CHART 1-21
YIELD PER HARVESTED ACRE FOR COTTON, CORN, WHEAT AND SOYBEANS IN THE UNITED STATES, 1920, 1930, 1940, and 1948-74

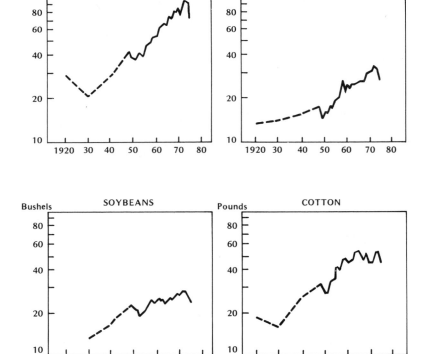

Source: For tabulation of data, see Table 1-3.

Table 1-3

YIELD PER HARVESTED ACRE FOR COTTON, CORN,
WHEAT, AND SOYBEANS IN THE UNITED STATES,
1920, 1930, 1940, and 1948-74

Year	Cotton (lb.)	Corn (bu)	Wheat (bu)	Soy-beans (bu)
1920	187	29.9	13.5	--
1930	157	20.5	14.2	13.0
1940	253	28.9	15.3	16.2
1948	311	43.0	17.9	21.3
1949	282	38.2	14.5	22.3
1950	269	38.2	16.5	21.7
1951	269	36.9	16.0	20.8
1952	280	41.8	18.4	20.7
1953	324	40.7	17.3	18.2
1954	341	39.4	18.1	20.0
1955	417	42.0	19.8	20.1
1956	409	47.4	20.2	21.8
1957	388	48.3	21.8	23.2
1958	466	52.8	27.5	24.2
1959	461	53.1	21.6	23.5
1960	446	54.1	26.1	23.5
1961	438	62.4	23.9	25.1
1962	457	64.7	25.0	24.2
1963	517	67.9	25.2	24.4
1964	517	62.9	25.8	22.8
1965	527	74.1	26.5	24.5
1966	480	73.1	26.3	25.4
1967	447	80.1	25.8	24.5
1968	516	79.5	28.4	26.7
1969	434	85.9	30.6	27.4
1970	438	72.4	31.0	26.7
1971	438	88.1	33.9	27.5
1972	507	97.1	32.7	27.8
1973	519	91.4	31.7	27.8
(1974)*	(438)	(72.5)	(27.4)	(23.7)

*Preliminary estimate.

SOURCES

U.S. Department of Agriculture, Agricultural Statistics, 1972 (Washington, D.C.:
U.S. Government Printing Office, 1973); USDA, Agricultural Statistics, 1974.

R&D and the Productivity Growth of Industries

Chart 1-22 shows the growth in total factor productivity (output
relative to an index combining labor and physical capital) in the

CHART 1-22

AVERAGE OF THE TOTAL FACTOR PRODUCTIVITY INDEXES OF INDUSTRY GROUPS WITH HIGH, MEDIUM AND LOW 1958 PRIVATE R&D INTENSITY RATIOS OF COMBINED DIRECT R&D EXPENDITURE AND R&D ATTRIBUTED TO PURCHASED IN-PUTS, 1948-66 (Based on data for 33 industries, 1948 = 100)

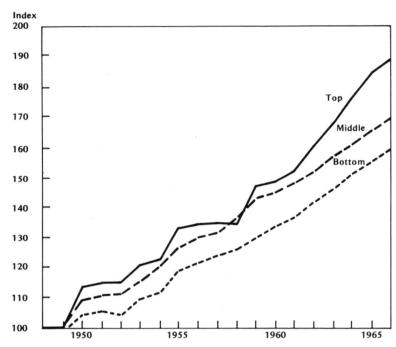

GROUPING OF INDUSTRIES BY THE RATIO OF COMBINED R&D TO VALUE ADDED (1958 RATIOS)

Top Third	%	Middle Third	%	Bottom Third	%
Transportation equip. and ordnance	10.7	Stone, clay and glass products, etc.	1.4	Metal mining	0.4
Chemicals	8.6	Fabricated metals	1.4	Apparel	0.4
Electrical machinery	7.4	Farming	1.1	Leather	0.4
Instruments	6.3	Food, etc.	1.1	Water trans.	0.4
Petroleum refining	5.2	Communication util.	0.9	Coal mining	0.3
Machinery, exc. electrical	4.8	Furniture	0.6	Oil and gas	0.3
Rubber	3.4	Beverages	0.6	Tobacco	0.3
Textiles	2.5	Contract construction	0.6	Railroads	0.2
Airlines	1.6	Lumber	0.5	Printing & publishing	0.2
Primary metals	1.5	Electric and gas util.	0.4	Wholesale trade	0.1
Paper	1.4	Nonmetallic mining	0.4	Retail trade	0.1

Source: For tabulation of data, see Table 1-4.

industries for which such productivity data are available, arranged into three groups according to the level of their "combined" R&D intensity, reflecting direct and indirect R&D. This ratio of R&D intensity to value added (1) does not include the cost of government financed R&D performance (except for agriculture), and (2) includes, in addition to the cost of the privately financed R&D performed in the industry, the estimated amounts of privately financed R&D "embodied" in the purchases of intermediate and capital goods from other industries which conduct R&D. This indirect R&D was attributed to the purchasing industries in proportion to sales.

Industries with higher combined R&D intensity had, on the average, higher rates of productivity growth. The growth rate of total factor productivity in the period 1948 to 1966 in the group with highest R&D intensity was 3.6 percent, in the middle R&D group 3.0 percent, and in the group with the lowest combined R&D ratio 2.6 percent. The productivity index for the high R&D group halted or even dipped below the index for the middle group in the years of economic recessions, evidently reflecting the preponderance of the recession-sensitive capital goods industries such as transportation equipment, electrical equipment, instruments and machinery.

The chart depicts the association between industrial R&D and productivity growth on a gross rather than a net basis. No adjustments were made for factors other than R&D that also influence productivity growth of industries.

General Interest Scientific Periodicals

Circulation of general scientific periodicals shows the extent to which scientific knowledge is being disseminated both within the scientific community between persons skilled in different disciplines and between the scientific community and segments of the general public. (No comparable data can be compiled for the broadcasting media, because neither the networks nor the regulatory agencies have classified the programs in any manner which would permit identification of those with a scientific content.)

Table 1-4

AVERAGE OF THE TOTAL FACTOR PRODUCTIVITY INDEXES OF INDUSTRY GROUPS WITH HIGH, MEDIUM AND LOW 1958 PRIVATE R&D INTENSITY RATIOS OF COMBINED DIRECT R&D EXPENDITURE AND R&D ATTRIBUTED TO PURCHASED INPUTS TO VALUE ADDED, 1948-66
(Based on data for 33 industries, 1948 = 100)

	1948	1949	1950	1951	1952	1953	1954	1955	1956	1957	1958	1959
Group with highest R&D intensity ratios	100.0	100.0	113.9	115.0	115.2	120.2	121.2	132.7	133.8	134.0	133.5	147.1
Group with medium R&D intensity ratios	100.0	101.6	109.2	110.2	110.4	115.1	120.1	126.7	129.2	131.6	135.7	142.5
Group with lowest R&D intensity ratios	100.0	98.2	105.0	106.0	104.5	109.1	111.3	118.6	121.2	123.5	125.2	129.3

	1960	1961	1962	1963	1964	1965	1966
Group with highest R&D intensity ratios	148.2	152.5	160.5	168.1	176.0	185.5	188.4
Group with medium R&D intensity ratios	144.2	148.2	151.8	157.3	160.7	165.1	168.8
Group with lowest R&D intensity ratios	132.7	135.8	140.8	145.2	150.8	155.0	159.3

SOURCES

For productivity: John W. Kendrick, Postwar Productivity Trends in the United States, 1948-1969, NBER General Series 98 (New York: National Bureau of Economic Research, 1973), pp. 254-355. For combined R&D intensity: Nestor E. Terleckyj, Effects of R&D on the Productivity Growth of Industries: An Exploratory Study (Washington, D.C.: National Planning Association, December 1974), pp. 13 and 15.

CHART 1-23

AVERAGE U.S. CIRCULATION OF THE GENERAL INTEREST
SCIENTIFIC PERIODICALS

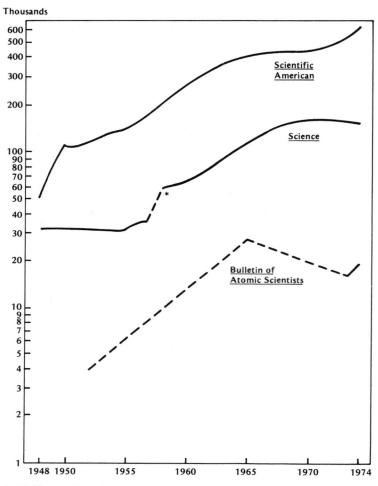

* In 1958, Science combined with The Scientific Monthly.

Source: For tabulation of data, see Table 1-5.

Table 1-5

AVERAGE U.S. CIRCULATION OF THE
GENERAL INTEREST SCIENTIFIC PERIODICALS
(In thousands)

Year	Science	Scientific American	The Bulletin of the Atomic Scientists
1948	32	50	–
1949	32	83	–
1950	32	109	–
1951	33	108	–
1952	32	119	4
1953	31	124	–
1954	31	130	–
1955	32	138	–
1956	35	154	–
1957	37	174	–
1958	59	207	–
1959	61	239	–
1960	63	272	–
1961	70	299	–
1962	77	331	–
1963	90	359	–
1964	101	385	–
1965	112	407	27
1966	125	414	–
1967	135	421	–
1968	140	421	–
1969	149	434	–
1970	158	451	–
1971	162	446	–
1972	154	464	–
1973	155	527	16
1974	152	581	18

SOURCE

Data provided by the National Planning Association.

Part II

NEW INDICATORS FOR R&D ACTIVITIES

2 The Number of Scientists and Engineers in Basic Research: An Indicator of the Level of Scientific Activity

Rory Paredes

Introduction

While technological applications of science can be measured by the total level of applied research and development expenditures, the core of scientific activities is best measured by the level of effort—in real terms—in basic research. As an indicator chosen to represent the real (as distinct from monetary) level of scientific effort, scientific manpower engaged in basic research was considered preferable to a measure based on expenditures or on total manpower in basic research. The latter would introduce relative salary trends and the use of supporting personnel and other inputs into the measure, diluting its significance as an index of scientific activity. Although the choice made does not preclude problems of ignoring such factors as worker productivity, modification of skill levels, organizational changes and other qualitative factors, the result would still be a useful indicator of volume to complement available expenditure data. The estimates developed for this purpose are time series showing basic research professional scientific employment, estimated from related expenditure, and R&D employment data and the number of doctoral scientists and engineers engaged in basic research, as reported by surveys.

The Estimates

Table 2-1 shows that the number of scientists and engineers engaged in basic research grew from 27,000 in 1954 to 42,000 in 1958, increasing further to a peak of 87,000 in 1969 and declining thereafter to 78,000 in 1973. These trends, of course, differ from the growth in (undeflated) basic research expenditures, which increased continuously and grew over 700 percent from 1954 to 1973 (see Appendix Table 2-1).

TABLE 2-1

ESTIMATED NUMBER OF SCIENTISTS AND ENGINEERS AND OF DOCTORAL
SCIENTISTS AND ENGINEERS ENGAGED IN BASIC RESEARCH, U.S. TOTAL,
SELECTED YEARS,1953-73
(In thousands of full-time equivalent man-years)

Year	Total Scientists and Engineers	Doctoral Scientists and Engineers* Reported in Survey	Estimated Total
1954	27	...	...
...	...	...	...
1958	42	...	...
...	...	...	...
1960	...	17	23
1961	55	...	...
1962	...	18	24
...	...	...	...
1964	...	20	27
1965	74	...	...
1966	...	23	31
...	...	...	...
1968	85	27	36
1969	87	...	...
1970	86	27	36
1971	82		...
1972	80	dis- cont'd	31
1973	78		...

*The years reported, 1960 to 1970, exclude engineers; separate data for basic research
are not available, but in 1972, we estimate engineers were approximately 32 thousand
or 6 percent of the total 526 thousand of doctoral scientists and engineers in all R&D
activities.

The total series consist of the numbers reported in the survey adjusted for coverage
for the years 1966-70 and the estimate of the National Academy of Science for 1972.
The coverage adjustment of the reported number of doctoral scientists necessary to
make the NSF survey data more nearly comparable to the NAS estimate of the total
number consists of dividing the NSF survey series by a factor of 0.75 which represents
an expert judgment of the coverage difference between the two estimates.

Sources: Basic research employment was estimated from R&D expenditure and employment, National Science Foundation, National Patterns of R&D Resources, Funds and
Manpower in the United States, 1953-74, NSF 74-304 (Washington, D.C.: U.S. Govern-
ment Printing Office, 1974), Tables B-1, B-2 and B-10, pp 20 ff; doctorate level employ-
ment data are from the National Register of Scientific and Technical Personnel,
American Science Manpower, 1960-1970 surveys, and the National Academy of Sciences,
Doctoral Scientists and Engineers in the United States, 1973 Profile (Washington, D.C.,
March 1974).

For the period in which the data on doctoral scientists are
available (1961-70), employment of doctoral degree holders
grew at a yearly rate of 5.9 percent while the number of all
scientists and engineers in basic research increased at a slightly
higher rate of 6.1 percent. These rates exceed the growth of R&D
scientific employment of an average 4.1 percent during this
period.

Basic research has been performed largely by colleges and universities, a specialization which has remained unchanged over the past two decades (see Table 2-2). The academic sector accounted for 50-60 percent of all basic research professional scientific employment from 1954 to 1973, and this percentage has increased.

TABLE 2-2

ESTIMATED NUMBER OF SCIENTISTS AND ENGINEERS ENGAGED IN BASIC RESEARCH, TOTAL AND BY SECTOR
(In thousands)

Year	All Fields	Sector				
		Federal Government	Private Industry	Colleges & Univ.'s	Assoc. FFRDC's	Nonprofit Institutions
1954	27	4	7	14	1	1
...	...	...	...	...	...	...
1958	42	4	9	24	2	3
...	...	...	...	...	...	...
1961	55	6	11	31	3	4
...	...	...	...	...	...	...
1965	74	9	15	40	4	6
1968	85	10	14	51	4	6
1969	86	11	13	53	4	5
1970	86	12	13	53	4	4
1971	82	9	12	52	4	4
1972	80	9	11	50	4	5
1973	78	9	13	46	4	6

Note: Numbers may not add to total due to rounding.

Source: Estimated from R&D expenditure and employment data, National Patterns of R&D Resources, Funds and Manpower in the United States, 1953-74, NSF 74-304 (Washington, D.C.: U.S. Government Printing Office, 1974), Tables B-1, B-2 and B-10, pp. 20-23 and 30.

Associated FFRDCs[1] and nonprofit institutions employed only about a thousand scientists and engineers for basic research activities in 1954. By 1973, associated FFRDCs' employment increased to about 4,000 and nonprofit institutions to 6,000 scientists and engineers. The trends in the two indicators are shown graphically in Chart 2-1.

Methodology

The absence of a series for scientists and engineers engaged in basic scientific research probably is the historical result of the difficulties of identifying basic research scientists and also a result of a preoccupation with R&D as an entity rather than as a collection of related components. Construction of a series now depends upon utilization of related series, such as R&D expenditures and scientific and technical manpower.

47

CHART 2-1

ESTIMATED NUMBER OF SCIENTISTS AND ENGINEERS AND OF
DOCTORAL SCIENTISTS AND ENGINEERS ENGAGED IN BASIC
RESEARCH, U.S. TOTAL, SELECTED YEARS, 1954-73

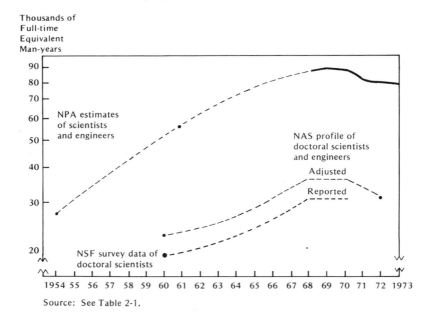

Source: See Table 2-1.

Accordingly, the estimates of scientists and engineers engaged in basic research are based on the ratio: *basic research expenditures to total R&D expenditures applied to total R&D scientists and engineers for each reported performing sector* (i.e., federal government, private industry, colleges and universities, federally funded R&D centers and miscellaneous nonprofit institutions).

Total and basic research expenditures by sector are reported in the National Science Foundation's *National Patterns of R&D Resources* for the period 1953-74,[2] and are based upon periodic surveys of the several sectors. The data appear reasonably complete, although social science expenditures are omitted in the private industry series.

Total R&D scientists and engineers are also reported in *National Patterns* on the full-time equivalent (FTE) concept, which provides a more satisfactory comparison with expenditure data than

48

the "primarily employed as" measures. Utilization of the Bureau of Labor Statistics series of R&D scientists and engineers was considered,[3] but the reporting basis of "primarily employed as" in this series is less consistent with the expenditure data than the FTE concept. Furthermore, the series covers a shorter period (1950-70). Unfortunately, the NSF data exclude scientists engaged in social science research in private industry as well as scientists and engineers employed by state and local government agencies. Neither exclusion is a major one.

The methodology for estimating basic research manpower implies a more or less consistent relationship between basic research and total R&D expenditures over time within performing sectors. Although the aggregate applied research and development components of R&D may be expected to contain a smaller professional manpower element than basic research, this effect is minimized when estimates are prepared individually by sector and then summed.

The companion estimates of doctoral scientists engaged in basic research for the period 1960-70 are as reported in the NSF *American Science Manpower* series. This series, representing survey data from the National Register, is incomplete in coverage. Each two-year registration was independently conducted, and it excludes doctoral engineers. The coverage of doctoral scientists has been estimated in the 70-80 percent range, although varying somewhat by discipline and type of employer. The 1972 estimate is derived from the National Academy of Sciences (NAS) sample from the Roster of Doctoral Scientists and Engineers, which achieved 75-80 percent response rates. This datum follows the "primarily employed as" concept, which, although less satisfactory for the purpose at hand, holds a promise of continuity for future series.

The data for doctoral scientists engaged in basic research should not be considered a continuous series. Not only are doctoral engineers excluded from National Register data and included in NAS data, but the latter represent a controlled sample from which improved estimates are possible. Adjustment of National Register coverage to allow for under-reporting is perhaps possible, but beyond the scope of this work.

APPENDIX TABLE 2-1

EXPENDITURES FOR R&D AND BASIC RESEARCH IN THE UNITED STATES, TOTAL AND BY SECTOR, 1954-73
(In thousands of dollars)

Year	Total R&D	Total BR	Federal Government R&D	Federal Government BR	Private Industry R&D	Private Industry BR	Colleges & Univ.'s R&D	Colleges & Univ.'s BR	Assoc. FFRDC's R&D	Assoc. FFRDC's BR	Nonprofit Institutions R&D	Nonprofit Institutions BR
1954	$5,738	$ 548	$1,020	$ 102	$4,070	$166	$ 377	$ 206	$141	$39	$ 130	$35
1958	10,870	973	1,374	126	8,389	295	592	390	293	78	222	84
1961	14,552	1,543	1,874	206	10,908	395	969	701	410	115	391	126
1965	20,439	2,853	3,093	424	14,185	592	1,822	1,419	629	208	710	210
1968	25,119	3,648	3,493	502	17,429	642	2,599	2,011	719	276	879	217
1969	26,169	3,758	3,501	565	18,318	618	2,695	2,087	725	275	930	213
1970	26,545	3,943	3,853	646	18,062	629	2,835	2,194	737	269	1,058	205
1971	27,336	4,000	4,156	535	18,332	625	3,070	2,355	716	260	1,062	225
(prel.) 1972	29,209	4,237	4,496	607	19,521	625	3,327	2,510	764	250	1,100	245
(est.) 1973	30,630	4,434	4,650	615	20,450	705	3,615	2,558	815	286	1,100	270

Source: NSF, National Patterns of R&D Resources, Tables B-1 and B-2, pp. 20-23.

APPENDIX TABLE 2-2

EMPLOYMENT OF R&D SCIENTISTS AND ENGINEERS BY SECTOR: 1954-73
(In thousands of full-time-equivalent man-years)

Year	Total	Federal Government	Private Industry	Colleges & Univ.'s	Assoc. FFRDC's	Nonprofit Institutions
1954	263.8	37.4	164.1	25.0	5.0	5.3
...	...	...	...	...	...	...
1958	354.7	46.1	256.1	36.5	8.1	7.9
...	...	...	...	...	...	...
1961	425.2	50.6	312.0	42.4	9.1	11.1
...	...	...	...	...	...	...
1965	496.5	64.2	348.4	53.4	11.1	19.4
1968	550.6	68.3	381.9	66.0	11.2	23.2
1969	559.2	70.3	385.6	68.3	11.6	23.4
1970	547.4	69.5	375.4	68.5	11.5	22.5
1971	528.9	68.5	359.5	68.4	11.5	21.0
1972	525.8	68.0	357.3	66.5	12.0	22.0
1973	531.1	65.8	365.2	64.6	12.5	23.0

Source: NSF, National Patterns of R&D Resources, Table B-10, p. 30.

Notes

1 FFRDCs are federally funded research and development centers administered by individual universities and colleges and by university consortia.

2 National Science Foundation, *National Patterns of R&D Resources, Funds and Manpower in the United States, 1953-74,* NSF 74-304 (Washington, D.C.: U.S. Government Printing Office, 1974).

3 Bureau of Labor Statistics, U.S. Department of Labor, *Employment of Scientists and Engineers 1950-70,* Bulletin 1781 (Washington, D.C.: U.S. Government Printing Office, 1973).

3 The Domestic Stock of Research and Development Capital in the United States: A Sensitivity Analysis for the Period 1948-76

Neil J. McMullen and Ivars Zageris

Introduction

This chapter estimates, under various assumptions, the stock of domestic research and development capital from 1948 to 1977. The calculation for a given year represents the data for a period ending three years earlier because, for each estimate, a three-year lag is assumed between R&D expenditure and its embodiment in R&D capital. This is an exploratory work and results are to be considered highly experimental.

Most discussions of state of science are based on the time series of annual research and development activity, such as the national expenditure of R&D, the ratio of R&D expenditure to GNP, or the number of scientists, engineers and supporting staff engaged in R&D activities. These data have provided basic information for resource allocation decisions and for judgments regarding the employment conditions of scientists and engineers. The data have also been taken as a proxy for output measure which is not available for R&D. As such, they can be interpreted as the quantity of new research knowledge produced during the period. It is a valid concept in this role to the extent that the assumption equating input and output can be accepted; but, as a principal indicator of the state of research activity, the data are incomplete because they relate only to the increments of knowledge and do not describe the stock of knowledge. The latter, of course, is difficult to measure, but the annual increment by itself is not a good indicator of the rate at which the research knowledge in the nation or in any given field or industry is growing or how large the accumulated stock may be. The rate of growth in research manpower or deflated expenditures does not indicate the rate at which the stock or the amount of scientific knowledge is growing. Yet, all the theories at least, of the economic impact of R&D are predicated on the notion of intangible R&D capital. This notion has given rise to the estimates of intangible R&D capital by John Kendrick and Leonore Wagner and has been used by a number of researchers in the field, notably Edwin Mansfield and Zvi Griliches.[1] Measurement of R&D capital is extremely difficult, but enough attempts have been made in the past to warrant an experimental attempt to compound past R&D investments into a capital stock series. This requires some assumptions about the depreciation rate of R&D investments and about the time lag between the conduct of research and its embodiment in the stock of useful knowledge.

The appropriate concept for investments would be applied R&D. But because the data for basic and applied research are not readily separable and since basic research activity has absorbed only a small proportion (about 6 or 7 percent) of the total R&D resources, total R&D investment inputs are used in this chapter. Also, because deflation for price changes raises very difficult conceptual and statistical problems, R&D man-years of scientists and engineers engaged in research and development are used as the national total R&D investment series. However, a series of capital stock estimates based upon privately financed R&D expenditures were calculated. This series probably comes much closer to the concept of a capital stock than the series based on total U.S. man-years.

Capital Stock Estimates of Total U.S. R&D Man-years

Basic Data Series

The basic data (see Table 3-1 or Chart 3-1) for the estimation of the domestic stock of R&D capital for the United States were obtained from the National Science Foundation, *National Patterns of R&D Resources.*[2] For the period preceding 1954, use was made of the data in Terleckyj's Conference Board publication as a form of benchmark.[3] Terleckyj's data was linked to the NSF data. Using Terleckyj's data for the years 1921, 1931, 1940, 1946 and 1951, a curve was fitted to the benchmark and an estimate of the man-years of scientists and engineers engaged in research and development for each year over the period 1921 to 1973 was made.

TABLE 3-1

ESTIMATED MAN-YEARS OF SCIENTISTS AND ENGINEERS ENGAGED
IN RESEARCH AND DEVELOPMENT IN THE UNITED STATES, 1921-74
(In thousands)

Year	Man-Years	Year	Man-Years	Year	Man-Years
1921	20**	1939	67	1957	323
1922	21	1940	71**	1958	355*
1923	23	1941	76	1959	377
1924	24	1942	82	1960	401
1925	26	1943	88	1961	426*
1926	28	1944	94	1962	442
1927	30	1945	101	1963	459
1928	32	1946	109**	1964	476
1929	34	1947	117	1965	494*
1930	37	1948	125	1966	511
1931	41**	1949	134	1967	538
1932	44	1950	143	1968	550*
1933	46	1951	153**	1969	558*
1934	49	1952	178	1970	550*
1935	52	1953	205	1971	529*
1936	56	1954	237*	1972	522*
1937	59	1955	262	1973	523*
1938	63	1956	291	1974	528*

*National Science Foundation, National Patterns of R&D Resources,
Funds and Manpower in the United States, 1953-74, NSF 74-304 (Washington,
D.C.: U.S. Government Printing Office, 1974), Table B-10.

**Nestor E. Terleckyj, Research and Development: Its Growth and Compo-
sition, Studies in Business Economics, No. 82 (New York: National Industrial Conference Board, 1963), Table A-3, p. 102.

Terleckyj's figures were adjusted to be compatible with the NSF series
in the following manner: (NSF's 1954 Figure/Terleckyj's 1954 Figure) X
Terleckyj's data. Data for all other years were geometrically interpolated.

In the NSF publication, the number of scientists and engineers
are measured on a full-time equivalent (FTE) basis, which provides a common denominator for combining the number of full-
time employees with a FTE number of part-time employees to
achieve a quantitative measure of manpower input. This measure
corresponds to the "man-year" concept.

The minimum standard for inclusion of scientists and engineers
was the performance of professional scientific and engineering
work in research and development, requiring a bachelor's
degree or its equivalent in science or engineering.

CHART 3-1

ESTIMATED MAN-YEARS OF SCIENTISTS AND ENGINEERS EN-
GAGED IN RESEARCH AND DEVELOPMENT IN THE UNITED
STATES, 1921-74

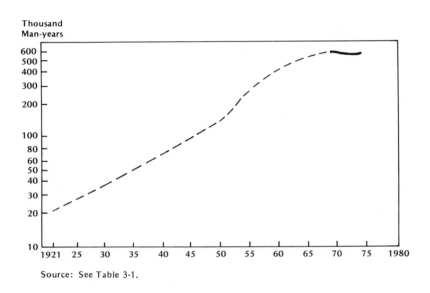

Source: See Table 3-1.

Estimates of R&D Stock

Estimates of the capital stock of man-years engaged in research
and development activity by scientists and engineers for the
years 1948 to 1977 are provided in Table 3-2 and graphically in
Chart 3-2. Depending upon the depreciation rate assumed, the
R&D capital stock ranges form a low of 2,580 thousand man-years
to a high of 11,991 thousand man-years by the end of 1977.
Because R&D investments were assumed to enter the stock of
R&D with a three-year lag, the cumulative data as of the end of
1973 appear under the date 1976.

The assumption that R&D investments would be embodied in the
capital stock after three years is based on research conducted by
Wagner, Raines and the McGraw-Hill Company.[4] Wagner takes
the position that all applied research and development is applied
within three years, with about 46 percent applied in the final
year. Raines suggests an average lag of 3.5 to 4.6 years between
R&D activity and large-scale production. Basic research would

56

TABLE 3-2 CAPITAL STOCK OF MAN-YEARS WORKED BY SCIENTISTS AND ENGINEERS ENGAGED IN RESEARCH AND DEVELOPMENT
ASSUMING A THREE-YEAR LAG AND DIFFERENT STRAIGHT LINE DEPRECIATION RATES IN THE UNITED STATES, 1948-77 (In thousands)

Year	Annual Gross Investment Lagged 3 Years	Zero Depreciation Capital Stock	Zero Depreciation Net Investment	2% Depreciation Capital Stock	2% Depreciation Net Investment	5% Depreciation Capital Stock	5% Depreciation Net Investment	10% Depreciation Capital Stock	10% Depreciation Net Investment	20% Depreciation Capital Stock	20% Depreciation Net Investment
1948	101	1,475	101	1,183	79	900	59	636	41	399	26
1949	109	1,584	109	1,268	85	964	64	681	45	429	30
1950	117	1,701	117	1,360	92	1,032	68	730	49	460	31
1951	125	1,826	125	1,458	98	1,106	74	782	52	493	33
1952	134	1,960	134	1,563	105	1,185	79	838	56	528	35
1953	143	2,103	143	1,674	111	1,268	83	897	59	566	38
1954	153	2,256	153	1,794	120	1,358	90	961	64	606	40
1955	178	2,434	178	1,936	142	1,468	110	1,042	81	662	56
1956	205	2,639	205	2,102	166	1,600	132	1,143	101	735	73
1957	237	2,876	237	2,297	195	1,757	157	1,266	123	825	90
1958	262	3,138	262	2,513	216	1,931	174	1,401	135	922	97
1959	291	3,429	291	2,754	241	2,125	194	1,552	151	1,029	107
1960	323	3,752	323	3,022	268	2,342	217	1,720	168	1,146	117
1961	355	4,107	355	3,316	294	2,580	238	1,903	183	1,272	126
1962	377	4,484	377	3,627	311	2,828	248	2,090	187	1,394	122
1963	401	4,885	401	3,956	329	3,088	260	2,282	192	1,516	122
1964	426	5,311	426	4,302	346	3,359	271	2,480	198	1,639	123
1965	442	5,753	442	4,658	356	3,633	274	2,674	194	1,753	114
1966	459	6,212	459	5,024	366	3,911	278	2,865	191	1,862	109
1967	476	6,688	476	5,400	376	4,191	280	3,055	190	1,965	103
1968	494	7,182	494	5,786	386	4,475	284	3,243	188	2,066	101
1969	511	7,693	511	6,181	395	4,763	288	3,430	187	2,164	98
1970	538	8,231	538	6,595	414	5,063	300	3,625	195	2,269	105
1971	550	8,781	550	7,013	418	5,359	296	3,812	187	2,365	96
1972	558	9,339	558	7,431	418	5,649	290	3,989	177	2,450	85
1973	550	9,889	550	7,832	401	5,917	268	4,140	151	2,510	60
1974	529	10,418	529	8,205	373	6,150	233	4,255	115	2,537	27
1975	522	10,940	522	8,563	358	6,365	215	4,352	97	2,552	15
1976	523	11,463	523	8,915	352	6,569	204	4,440	88	2,564	12
1977	528	11,991	528	9,264	349	6,769	200	4,524	84	2,580	16

Source: Based upon Table 3-1.

CHART 3-2

CAPITAL STOCK OF R&D MAN-YEARS WORKED BY
SCIENTISTS AND ENGINEERS ENGAGED IN R&D ASSUMING
DIFFERENT STRAIGHT LINE DEPRECIATION RATES AND A
THREE-YEAR LAG, UNITED STATES, 1948-77

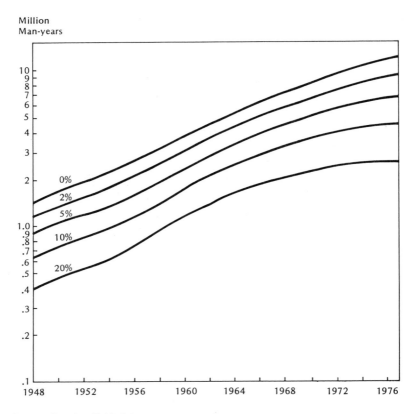

Million
Man-years

Source: Based on Table 3-1.

presumably take even longer to be assimilated into the stock of production R&D capital.

In the 1968 annual McGraw-Hill survey, 90 percent of all the firms cooperating expected their R&D in pay off in two years or less. Only 4 percent of the firms indicated that they expected to wait 10 years or more for a payoff from R&D.

Since all of the estimates are based upon a three-year lag, the basis for the wide difference in estimates (ranging from 2,580 thousand to 11,991 thousand in 1977) is the different depreciation rates assumed, which range from zero to 20 percent per year on a straight line basis.

Griliches states that scattered evidence on the longevity of research results suggests that a depreciation rate of about 10 percent per annum may not be out of line.[5] In his study, Mansfield assumes depreciation rates of 4 percent and 7 percent.[6] Considerable research will be needed to determine the "actual" depreciation rate. Straight line depreciation was assumed here for simplicity's sake.

Growth Patterns

Table 3-3 indicates, for selected periods, the annual growth rates of yearly R&D capital investment and the five estimates of R&D capital stock. The yearly R&D capital investment growth rate starts to decline in the periods after 1962.

The annual growth rates of the different estimates of R&D capital stock also declined after 1962, but not as much.

TABLE 3-3

ANNUAL GROWTH OF YEARLY GROSS R&D INVESTMENT
AND ACCUMULATED R&D INVESTMENT BASED ON MAN-YEARS OF
R&D SCIENTISTS AND ENGINEERS UNDER DIFFERENT
DEPRECIATION ASSUMPTIONS FOR SELECTED TIME PERIODS
(In percentages)

Time period	Annual growth of yearly R&D investment	Annual growth of R&D capital stock based upon different depreciation assumptions				
		Depreciation				
		Zero	2%	5%	10%	20%
1948-74	6.6%	8.4%	8.2%	8.1%	7.8%	7.4%
1948-62	9.9	8.3	8.3	8.5	8.9	9.4
1962-69	4.4	8.0	7.9	7.7	7.3	6.5
1969-74	0.7	6.2	5.8	5.3	4.4	3.2

Table 3-4 indicates for different years of the period what proportion of the yearly R&D investment is needed to replace losses due to depreciation. The remaining proportion represents a net increase in R&D capital stock. The differences in the proportion of replacement investment are very large depending on the depreciation assumptions. If the depreciation rate of R&D

TABLE 3-4

RATIO OF ANNUAL R&D NET INVESTMENT TO ANNUAL R&D GROSS
INVESTMENT ASSUMING DIFFERENT DEPRECIATION RATES
IN THE UNITED STATES, 1948-77
(In percentages)

Year	Zero Depreciation	2% Depreciation	5% Depreciation	10% Depreciation	20% Depreciation
1948	100%	78%	58%	41%	26%
1949		78	59	41	28
1950		79	58	42	26
1951		78	59	42	26
1952		78	59	42	26
1953		78	58	41	27
1954		78	59	42	26
1955		80	62	46	31
1956		81	64	49	36
1957		82	66	52	38
1958		82	66	52	37
1959		83	67	52	37
1960		83	67	52	36
1961		83	67	52	35
1962		82	66	50	32
1963		82	65	48	30
1964		81	64	46	29
1965		81	62	44	26
1966		80	61	42	24
1967		79	59	40	22
1968		78	57	38	20
1969		77	56	37	19
1970		77	56	36	20
1971		76	54	34	17
1972		75	52	32	15
1973		73	49	27	11
1974		71	44	22	5
1975		69	41	19	3
1976		67	39	17	2
1977	100%	66%	38%	16%	3%

Source: Derived from Table 3-2.

is 5 percent or more, currently at least 70 percent of the yearly
R&D investment is needed for replacement.

Capital Stock Estimates of Privately Financed Industrial R&D Expenditures

Method

Business expenditure for R&D corresponds more closely to the
concepts of investment and capital than the national total R&D
expenditure or man-years. A series of (private) R&D capital in
industry is constructed using annual data for private expenditures for industrial R&D in constant dollars.

In order to construct the stock of R&D, the time series of annual

R&D expenditures have to be converted into constant dollars. However, no precise R&D price deflator exists. An R&D price deflator would have to take into consideration the distribution of cost for scientific personnel, supporting personnel, materials and supplies and other costs such as depreciation of the R&D capital used in the industry. However, the GNP price deflator was used here as an approximation for the R&D price deflator.

Time Lag

Since R&D is not a homogeneous product, several questions have to be considered about R&D investment. When does R&D investment enter the stock? When is R&D completed? And what proportion of prior years' expenditures must be added to the expenditures of R&D completed in a given year to derive the total value of R&D *entering* stock? As noted previously, we assumed here that the R&D expenditures would enter the capital stock after the three-year lag. The R&D investments were depreciated at rates ranging from 5 to 20 percent.

Real Annual Expenditure for Industrial R&D

The basic data were obtained from *National Patterns of R&D Resources.*[7] Only privately financed industrial R&D was used. Estimates of the cost of industrial R&D performance for selected years from 1921 to 1953 were made in a study by Terleckyj.[8]

These early estimates were adjusted to exclude government financed industrial R&D for the years 1940 to 1951 and the resulting series linked to the NSF data. Before 1940, all industrial R&D performed was assumed to be privately financed. In 1940, 95 percent of the industrial R&D performed was assumed to be privately financed; in 1946, 80 percent; and in 1951, 60 percent. The mean percentage for the years 1953 to 1973 is 55 percent. Table 3-5 and Chart 3-3 show the estimated amount of privately financed funds expended annually for performance of industrial research and development in the United States from 1921 to 1974.

Estimates of R&D Capital in Industry

Estimates of the R&D capital stock based upon R&D expenditures for the years 1948 to 1977 are provided in Table 3-6 and graphical-

TABLE 3-5

ESTIMATED CONSTANT DOLLAR ANNUAL EXPENDITURE BY PRIVATE
INDUSTRY FOR PERFORMANCE OF RESEARCH AND DEVELOPMENT,
UNITED STATES, 1921-74
(Millions of 1973 dollars)

Year	Expenditure	Year	Expenditure
1921*	$ 275	1948	$ 1,843
1922	300	1949	1,971
1923	330	1950	2,079
1924	365	1951*	2,324
1925	400	1952	2,824
1926	420	1953	3,912
1927*	460	1954	4,076
1928	500	1955	4,296
1929	525	1956	5,477
1930	596	1957	5,477
1931*	724	1958	5,711
1932	698	1959	6,159
1933*	628	1960	6,735
1934	659	1961	7,005
1935	735	1962	7,461
1936	830	1963	7,846
1937	895	1964	8,336
1938*	1,020	1965	9,102
1939	1,177	1966	9,910
1940*	1,306	1967	10,674
1941	1,372	1968	11,353
1942	1,412	1969	12,046
1943	1,520	1970	11,901
1944	1,698	1971	11,792
1945	1,889	1972	12,120
1946*	1,943	1973	12,880
1947	1,861	1974	12,876

*Benchmark year.

Sources: Years 1921, 1927, 1931, 1933, 1938, 1940, 1946, and 1951:
Nestor E. Terleckyj, "Research and Development: Its Growth and
Composition," Studies in Business Economics, No. 82 (New York: Na-
tional Industrial Conference Board, 1963), Table A-2, p. 100, adjusted
as described in text.   Years 1953-74: National Science Foundation,
National Patterns of R&D Resources, Funds and Manpower in the United
States, 1953-1974, NSF 74-304 (Washington, D.C.: U.S. Government
Printing Office, February 1974), Table B-5, p. 28. All other intervening
years' current dollar data were interpolated between benchmark years and
then deflated by the GNP deflator. See text for procedure.

CHART 3-3

ESTIMATED CONSTANT DOLLAR ANNUAL EXPENDITURE BY
PRIVATE INDUSTRY FOR PERFORMANCE OF RESEARCH AND
DEVELOPMENT, UNITED STATES, 1921-74

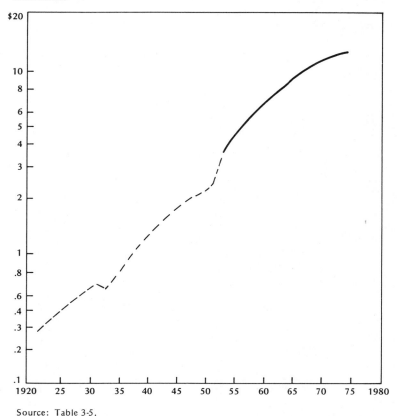

Source: Table 3-5.

ly in Chart 3-4. Depending upon the depreciation rate assumed, the private industry R&D capital stock in the United States ranges from a low of $58 billion to a high of $136 billion by the end of 1977. These estimates reflect the annual expenditures through the year 1974. The capital stock series extend to 1977 because R&D investments were assumed to enter the stock of R&D with a three-year lag.

TABLE 3-6

CAPITAL STOCK OF PRIVATELY FINANCED R&D EXPENDI-
TURES FOR PERFORMANCE OF INDUSTRIAL RESEARCH AND
DEVELOPMENT IN THE UNITED STATES, CUMULATED BY
ASSUMING A THREE-YEAR LAG AND DIFFERENT STRAIGHT
LINE DEPRECIATION RATES, 1948-77
(Billions of 1973 dollars)

Year	Depreciation Rates			
	5%	10%	15%	20%
1948	15.1	10.9	8.5	7.0
1949	16.3	11.7	9.2	7.6
1950	17.4	12.4	9.7	7.9
1951	18.3	13.0	10.1	8.2
1952	19.4	13.7	10.5	8.5
1953	20.5	14.4	11.0	8.9
1954	21.8	15.3	11.7	9.4
1955	23.5	16.6	12.8	10.4
1956	26.3	18.8	14.8	12.2
1957	29.0	21.0	16.6	13.8
1958	31.9	23.2	18.4	15.4
1959	35.8	26.4	21.1	17.8
1960	39.4	29.2	23.4	19.7
1961	43.2	32.0	25.6	21.5
1962	47.2	35.0	28.0	23.3
1963	51.6	38.2	30.5	25.4
1964	56.0	41.4	32.9	27.3
1965	60.6	44.7	35.4	29.3
1966	65.5	48.1	38.0	31.3
1967	70.5	51.6	40.6	33.4
1968	76.1	55.6	43.6	35.8
1969	82.2	59.9	47.0	38.6
1970	88.8	64.6	50.6	41.5
1971	95.7	69.5	54.4	44.6
1972	102.9	74.6	58.3	47.7
1973	109.7	79.0	61.4	50.1
1974	116.0	82.9	64.0	51.8
1975	122.3	86.7	66.5	53.6
1976	129.1	90.9	69.4	55.8
1977	135.5	94.7	71.9	57.5

Source: Based upon Table 3-5.

CHART 3-4

CAPITAL STOCK OF PRIVATELY FINANCED R&D EXPENDI-
TURES FOR PERFORMANCE OF INDUSTRIAL RESEARCH AND
DEVELOPMENT CUMULATED BY ASSUMING A THREE-YEAR
LAG AND DIFFERENT STRAIGHT LINE DEPRECIATION RATES,
UNITED STATES

Billions of
1973 Dollars

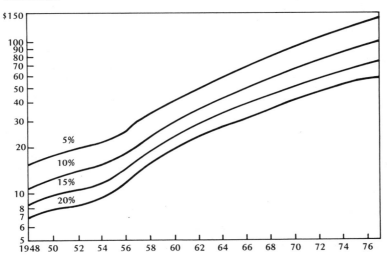

Source: See data in Table 3-6.

The present estimates based on the 5 percent depreciation are
similar to the estimates made by Wagner of gross business
applied R&D stock. Converted to 1973 dollars, she estimated the
1948 stock to be $14.8 billion, the 1958 stock to be $30.6 billion
and the 1966 stock to be $52.5 billion. The difference arises from
several factors. Wagner estimated applied only R&D stock. She
assumed that the applied R&D enters stock at the time it is put
into use. She incorporated different depreciation rates for dura-
ble and nondurable goods in her estimating procedure. All
applied R&D on nondurable goods was considered applied
within 30 months, with more than one-third incorporated during
the first year. All durable-goods applied R&D was considered
fully applied within three years, but with about 46 percent
applied during the final year. Furthermore, Wagner used her
own index for price deflation rather than the GNP deflator.[9]

Growth Patterns

Table 3-7 indicates, for selected periods, the average annual growth rates in the private business R&D capital. These growth rates declined after 1962.

TABLE 3-7

ANNUAL GROWTH OF YEARLY PRIVATELY FINANCED BUSINESS R&D EXPENDITURES AND ACCUMULATED R&D INVESTMENT BASED ON PRIVATELY FINANCED BUSINESS R&D EXPENDITURE UNDER DIFFERENT DEPRECIATION ASSUMPTIONS FOR SELECTED TIME PERIODS (In percentages)

Time period	Annual growth of yearly R&D investment	Annual growth of R&D capital stock based upon different depreciation assumptions			
		Depreciation			
		5%	10%	15%	20%
1948– 74	7.3%	8.2%	8.1%	8.1%	8.0%
1948– 62	8.8	8.5	8.7	8.9	9.0
1962– 69	7.0	8.2	8.0	7.7	7.5
1969– 74	3.5	7.1	6.7	6.4	6.1

Source: Derived from Tables 3-5 and 3-6.

Notes

1 John W. Kendrick, *Postwar Productivity Trends in the United States, 1948-1969* (New York: National Bureau of Economic Research, 1973); Leonore Wagner, "Problems in Estimating Research and Development Investment Stock," 1968 Proceedings of the Business and Economic Statistics Section (Washington, D.C.: American Statistical Association, 1968), pp. 189-198; Edwin Mansfield, *Industrial Research and Technological Innovation* (New York: W.W. Norton and Co., 1968), p. 30; Zvi Griliches, "Research Expenditures and Growth Accounting," *Science and Technology in Economic Growth,* ed. B.R. Williams, Proceedings of a Conference held by the International Economic Association at St. Anton, Austria (New York: John Wiley and Sons, Halstead Press, 1973).

2 National Science Foundation, *National Patterns of R&D Resources, Funds and Manpower in the United States, 1953-74*, NSF-74-304 (Washington, D.C.: U.S. Government Printing Office, 1974), Table B-10.

3 Nestor E. Terleckyj, "Research and Development: Its Growth and Composition," *Studies in Business Economics*, No. 82 (New York: National Industrial Conference Board, 1963), Table A-3, p. 102.

4 Wagner, "Problems in Estimating Research and Development," p. 192; Frederic Q. Raines, "The Impact of Applied Research and Development on Productivity," Working Paper No. 6814, presented at Sourthern Economic Association Meetings, Washington, D.C., November 1968; "Business' Plans for Research and Development Expenditures, 1968-1971," a McGraw-Hill survey, May 17, 1968.

5 Zvi Griliches, *The Measurement of Economic and Social Performance*, Studies in Income and Wealth, Vol. 38, ed., Milton Moss (New York: National Bureau of Economic Research, 1973), p. 434.

6 Mansfield, *Industrial Research and Technological Innovation*, p. 70.

7 NSF, *National Patterns of R&D Resources*, Table B-5.

8 Terleckyj, "Research and Development: Its Growth and Composition," Table A-2, p. 100.

9 Wagner, "Problems in Estimating Research and Development," pp. 192, 197.

4 Regional Distribution of Research and Development in the United States, 1964-73

Ivars Zageris

Introduction

Interest in the geographical dimension of research and development was stimulated originally by policy makers concerned with balance in the regional allocation of federal R&D funds between the use of the existing R&D capabilities on the one hand and a desire for an equal distribution of government funds and development of new R&D capabilities on the other. As a consequence, data has been accumulated over the past decade so that it is now possible to obtain some general indicators not only of government spending for R&D but also of the spatial dimension of industrial, governmental and academic R&D in the United States in general.

This chapter covers several dimensions of the geographical (regional) distribution of research and development. Specifically, it examines on a regional basis the per capita and total amounts of R&D expenditure in the United States for 1973; the regional trends in R&D performance from 1964 to 1973 by source of financing and the performing sector; and the regional patterns in industrial and academic R&D manpower. Included in the latter are the R&D scientists and engineers employed in industry for 1966 and the amount of time spent by teachers in the performance of teaching and R&D work, respectively, in colleges and universities in 1974.

The geographical dimension of R&D is examined in terms of large regions. These "census regions" and their respective states are listed in Table 4-1.

TABLE 4-1

THE NINE CENSUS REGIONS AND THEIR STATES

New England

Maine
New Hampshire
Vermont
Massachusetts
Rhode Island
Connecticut

Middle Atlantic

New York
New Jersey
Pennsylvania

East North Central

Ohio
Indiana
Illinois
Michigan
Wisconsin

South Atlantic

Delaware
Maryland
District of Columbia
Virginia
West Virginia
North Carolina
South Carolina
Georgia
Florida

East South Central

Kentucky
Tennessee
Alabama
Mississippi

West North Central

Minnesota
Iowa
Missouri
North Dakota
South Dakota
Nebraska
Kansas

West South Central

Arkansas
Louisiana
Oklahoma
Texas

Mountain

Montana
Idaho
Wyoming
Colorado
New Mexico
Arizona
Utah
Nevada

Pacific

Washington
Oregon
California
Alaska
Hawaii

The tables and charts that follow show, for the nine census regions, the total and per capita amounts of R&D expenditure in the United States. However, because the geography of research and development appears to be more interesting in its relation to the distribution of population, most tables and charts show the regional data on a per capita basis after the main absolute dimensions have been portrayed. The data used omit the relatively small amounts of the cost of R&D performed by nonprofit institutions (other than academic) and state governments, due to lack of data. The performing sectors for R&D expenditure are industry, federal government and colleges and universities. The financing sectors considered for R&D expenditure are industry and federal government.

Regional R&D Expenditure in the United States in 1973

Table 4-2 and Chart 4-1 show the distribution among the nine census regions of the total cost of research and development as performed by the federal government, industry and colleges and universities. The figures reported constitute the national total except for the comparatively small amounts spent for R&D conducted in nonacademic, nonprofit institutions and by state governments outside state universities. Such data were not available. Within the category of federal government is included work done by all federal government agencies. This work is carried out directly by the agencies' personnel. The per capita figures were derived by dividing the total R&D expenditure dollar amounts by the total resident population of the respective regions.

Approximately $28 billion was spent for the conduct of R&D in the United States in 1973. Column 2 of Table 4-2 and the top map of Chart 4-1 show how this $28 billion was distributed in absolute amounts among the nine regions. The largest share of R&D work was conducted in the Pacific region, namely, $6.3 billion. The Middle Atlantic, East North Central and South Atlantic regions followed with over $4 billion of R&D effort conducted in each.

Analytically, the degree of geographical dispersion of R&D activities can be more clearly perceived when portrayed relative to the distribution of population, i.e., on a per capita basis rather than in absolute amounts.

TABLE 4-2

TOTAL AND PER CAPITA EXPENDITURE FOR R&D
PERFORMANCE BY THE FEDERAL GOVERNMENT, INDUSTRY AND
COLLEGES AND UNIVERSITIES BY CENSUS REGION, 1973

Census Regions	Population (millions)	Total Cost of R&D Performed ($ billions)	Per Capita Cost of R&D Performed (dollars)
New England	12.2	$ 2.6	$213
Middle Atlantic	37.3	5.6	153
East North Central	40.9	5.5	135
South Atlantic	33.2	4.0	122
East South Central	13.4	0.7	56
West North Central	16.7	1.3	77
West South Central	20.6	1.1	53
Mountain	9.4	1.2	128
Pacific	27.8	6.3	232
UNITED STATES	211.5	$28.2	$135

SOURCES

National Science Foundation, Research and Development in Industry, 1973 (Washington, D.C.: U.S. Government Printing Office, 1975), Table 20; National Science Foundation, Science and Engineering Expenditures in Universities and Colleges, 1973 Selected Statistical Tables (Washington, D.C.: National Science Foundation, unpublished report), Table 7; National Science Foundation, Federal Funds for Research Development and Other Scientific Activities, Vols. 20 and 23 (Washington, D.C.: U.S. Government Printing Office, 1971 and 1974); Executive Office of the President, Council of Economic Advisers, Economic Report of the President (Washington, D.C.: U.S. Government Printing Office, 1974), Table C-3, p. 252; U.S. Department of Commerce, Bureau of the Census, Current Population Reports, Series P-25, No. 460, "Population Estimates and Projections" (Washington, D.C.: U.S. Government Printing Office, June 7, 1971), Table I, p. 8.

The per capita figures (column 3 of Table 4-2 and the bottom map of Chart 4-1) show a different geographical picture. First, since the distribution of population among regions correlates to some degree with the distribution of R&D, the range of variation among regions is reduced. The ratio of the largest amount of R&D conducted in a region to the lowest amount drops from 6 to 4 when measured on a per capita basis. Also, the relative preeminence of the New England states becomes apparent. These states and the Pacific region show the highest per capita expenditure while, as before, the East South Central and the West South Central regions show the lowest.

CHART 4-1

TOTAL AND PER CAPITA EXPENDITURE FOR R&D PERFOR-
MANCE BY THE FEDERAL GOVERNMENT, INDUSTRY AND
COLLEGES AND UNIVERSITIES BY CENSUS REGION, 1973

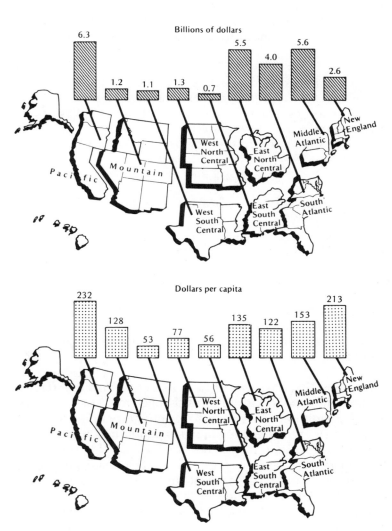

Source: Table 4-2.

Regional Trends in Per Capita Expenditure for R&D

The trend data on the geographical distribution of R&D are available for only the comparatively short period since the early 1960s. Chart 4-2 shows the per capita expenditure for R&D in the individual regions as well as in the United States as a whole, after deflating the R&D expenditure figures by the GNP price deflator. A more specific price index for the total R&D expenditure is not available.

The largest changes were a decline in the Pacific region (occurring between 1967 and 1970) and an increase in per capita R&D expenditure in New England (from 1964 to 1967). The West South Central region had a considerable percentage decline over the time period. Changes for other regions were relatively small in either direction.

Regional Patterns for Source of R&D Expenditure Financing

Table 4-3 and Chart 4-3 provide the regional patterns for federal or nonfederal (mostly industry) R&D expenditures. The data provide per capita figures which were deflated by the GNP price deflator. In some instances in constructing the series, the U.S. totals had been revised for former years in some of the newer publications. In those cases, the newer totals were used and the regional figures were recalculated by applying the former distribution to the newer totals.

The data show that the regional patterns have been rather stable. Governmental expenditure patterns changed more than those of private expenditure. Declines in government spending for R&D account for all of the decline in total expenditures in the Pacific and West South Central regions. Nonfederal R&D outlays in those two regions actually grew. The real private per capita expenditures increased in each of the nine regions while the federal expenditures declined in three and grew in one (New England) between 1964 and 1973, ignoring smaller changes in either direction. The largest absolute growth in the real private expenditure for R&D occurred in the East North Central region.

CHART 4-2
REGIONAL TRENDS IN PER CAPITA EXPENDITURE
FOR R&D PERFORMANCE, 1964-73 (in 1973 dollars)

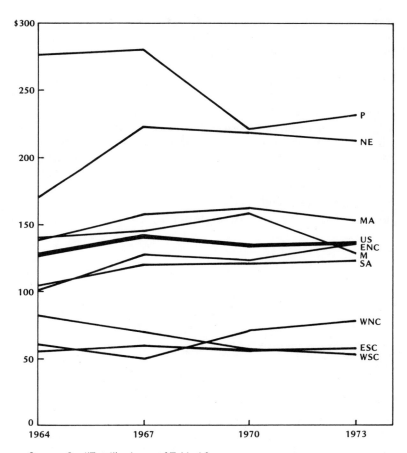

Source: See "Total" columns of Table 4-3.

Regional Patterns of R&D Performance by Sector

Table 4-4 and Chart 4-4 provide the regional patterns for per capita R&D expenditure in the United States by the R&D performing sectors for selected years from 1964 to 1973. (The data sources and the caveats are the same as for Table 4-3 and Chart 4-3.) The performing sectors for R&D expenditure are industry, federal government and colleges and universities. The data omit the relatively small amounts of R&D performed by nonacademic, nonprofit institutions and state governments (other than state universities) for which regional information is not available.

The data show that industrial performance accounts for most of the R&D activity in most regions with the single exception of the South Atlantic, which includes a substantial federal R&D establishment in the Maryland-Virginia-Washington, D.C. area and, to a lesser extent, in the Mountain region. The growth in R&D in the East North Central region was caused by the R&D performed in industry while the decline in R&D in the Pacific and West South Central regions also represent declines in industrial R&D. On the other hand, the slight growth in the South Atlantic region resulted from the growth in federally performed R&D. The

SOURCES FOR TABLE 4-3
National Science Foundation, Research and Development in Industry, 1973 (Washington, D.C.: U.S. Government Printing Office, 1975), Table 20; National Science Foundation, Research and Development in Industry, 1970, NSF 72-309 (Washington, D.C.: U.S. Government Printing Office, April 1972), Table 20, p. 52; National Science Foundation, Research and Development in Industry, 1967, NSF 69-28 (Washington, D.C.: U.S. Government Printing Office, July 1969), Table 21, p. 43; National Science Foundation, Research and Development in Industry, 1964, NSF 66-28 (Washington, D.C.: U.S. Government Printing Office, June 1966), Table 26, p. 36; National Science Foundation, Science and Engineering Expenditures in Universities and Colleges, 1973, Selected Statistical Tables (Washington, D.C.: National Science Foundation, unpublished report), Table 7; Committee on Science and Astronautics, U.S. House of Representatives, 88th Congress, 2nd Session, Obligations for Research and Development and R&D Plant, by Geographic Division and State, by Selected Federal Agencies, Fiscal Years 1961-1964 (Washington, D.C.: U.S. Government Printing Office, 1964), Table 4, pp. 36-37; National Science Foundation, Geographic Distribution of Federal Funds for FY 1965, NSF 67-8 (Washington, D.C.: U.S. Government Printing Office, 1965); National Science Foundation, Federal Funds for Research Development and Other Scientific Activities, Vols. 20 and 23 (Washington, D.C.: U.S. Government Printing Office, 1971 and 1974); Executive Office of the President, Council of Economic Advisers, Economic Report of the President, 1974 (Washington, D.C.: U.S. Government Printing Office, 1974), Table C-3, p. 252; and U.S. Department of Commerce, Bureau of the Census, Current Population Reports, Series P-25, No. 460, "Population Estimates and Projections" (Washington, D.C.: U.S. Government Printing Office, June 7, 1971), Table 1, p. 8, and Current Population Reports, Series P-20, No. 279, "Population Profile of the United States: 1974," Table 17, p. 23.

In some instances, the U.S. totals had been revised for former years in the newer publications. Those totals were used and the regional figures were calculated by applying the former distribution to the new totals.

TABLE 4-3
REGIONAL TRENDS IN PER CAPITA EXPENDITURE FOR R&D PERFORMANCE BY SOURCE OF FINANCING, 1964-73
(In 1973 dollars)

Census Regions / Financing Source	1964			1967			1970			1973		
	Federal	Non Federal	Total	Federal	Non Federal	Total	Federal	Non Federal	Total	Federal	Non Federal	Total
United States	$82	$47	$129	$85	$58	$143	$72	$63	$135	$70	$65	$135
New England	103	68	171	136	86	222	126	93	219	126	87	213
Middle Atlantic	64	75	139	71	86	157	67	95	162	58	95	153
East North Central	26	76	102	36	90	126	26	96	122	26	109	135
West North Central	36	24	60	21	29	50	32	39	71	39	38	77
South Atlantic	86	17	103	95	26	121	90	30	120	87	35	122
East South Central	44	12	56	45	13	58	42	13	55	42	14	56
West South Central	61	22	83	44	25	69	28	28	56	27	26	53
Mountain	120	21	141	114	31	145	112	46	158	92	36	128
Pacific	233	44	277	216	64	280	160	62	222	167	65	232

TABLE 4-4
REGIONAL TRENDS IN PER CAPITA EXPENDITURE FOR R&D PERFORMANCE BY PERFORMING SECTOR, 1964-73   (In 1973 dollars)

Regions	1964				1967				1970				1973			
	Industry	Federal Government	Colleges and Universities	Total	Industry	Federal Government	Colleges and Universities	Total	Industry	Federal Government	Colleges and Universities	Total	Industry	Federal Government	Colleges and Universities	Total
United States	$100	$25	$4	$129	$109	$29	$5	$143	$102	$28	$5	$135	$100	$31	$4	$135
New England	137	28	6	171	181	35	6	222	176	35	8	219	168	40	5	213
Middle Atlantic	119	16	4	139	134	18	5	157	138	18	6	162	131	18	4	153
East North Central	86	12	4	102	106	15	5	126	103	14	5	122	115	16	4	135
West North Central	49	6	5	60	35	9	6	50	55	10	6	71	62	10	5	77
South Atlantic	48	52	3	103	55	62	4	121	52	63	5	120	51	67	4	122
East South Central	34	19	3	56	28	27	3	58	30	22	3	55	28	26	2	56
West South Central	69	11	3	83	50	15	4	69	34	17	5	56	32	17	4	53
Mountain	84	51	6	141	80	58	7	145	98	52	8	158	69	53	6	128
Pacific	231	41	5	277	233	41	6	280	182	34	6	222	188	40	4	232

Source: See Sources for Table 4-3.

78

CHART 4-3

REGIONAL TRENDS IN PER CAPITA EXPENDITURE FOR R&D PERFORMANCE BY SOURCE OF FINANCING, 1964-73 (in 1973 dollars)

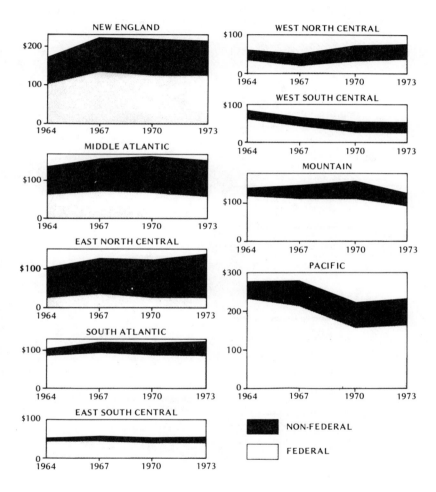

Source: See Table 4-3.

CHART 4-4

REGIONAL TRENDS IN PER CAPITA EXPENDITURE FOR R&D
PERFORMANCE BY PERFORMING SECTOR, 1964-73 (in 1973
dollars)

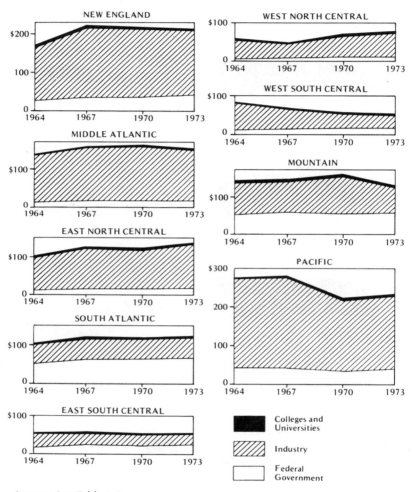

Source: See Table 4-3.

R&D efforts of colleges and universities have been rather small
when compared to the other two sectors, and they have been
rather stable.

Regional Distribution of Industrial R&D

Table 4-5 and Chart 4-5 show the regional deviations from the U.S. average in the number of scientists and engineers in industrial R&D per ten thousand workers in the labor force in 1966. The data on regional distribution of industrial R&D employment are presently available only for the years 1966 and 1969. The data for 1969 only cover 32 of the major R&D performing states.[1]

TABLE 4-5

REGIONAL DEVIATIONS FROM U.S. AVERAGE IN THE NUMBER OF SCIENTISTS AND ENGINEERS IN INDUSTRIAL RESEARCH AND DEVELOPMENT PER 10,000 WORKERS IN THE LABOR FORCE, 1966 (In thousands)

Region	Scientists	Engineers	Total
New England	+16	+10	+26
Middle Atlantic	+3	0	+3
East North Central	-2	+13	+11
West North Central	-5	-16	-21
South Atlantic	-4	-10	-14
East South Central	-6	-18	-24
West South Central	-5	-16	-21
Mountain	-8	-12	-20
Pacific	+6	+22	+28
U.S. Average	13	37	50

Sources: U.S. Department of Labor, Bureau of Labor Statistics, Scientific and Technological Personnel in Industry, 1961-1966, Bulletin No. 1609 (Washington, D.C.: U.S. Government Printing Office, 1968), Appendix 14a, p. 61. Labor force data are derived from U.S. Department of Labor, Statistics on Manpower, A Supplement to the Manpower Report of the President (Washington, D.C.: U.S. Government Printing Office, March 1969), Tables D1 and D3, pp. 58 and 60; also from U.S. Bureau of the Census, Statistical Abstract of the United States: 1967, 88th edition (Washington, D.C.: U.S. Government Printing Office, 1967), Table 345, p. 243.

The data show the distribution of the regional deviations from the U.S. average in the number of scientists and engineers in industrial R&D relative to the labor force. It shows numbers higher than the national average in the New England and Pacific regions and clearly lower in the Southern and Mountain regions. Especially pronounced is the relative concentration of scientists (as opposed to engineers) in the New England area, with engineers being slightly more concentrated, relatively, in the Pacific area. The Middle Atlantic region has a small relative concentration of scientists and the East North Central region has a slight concentration of engineers.

CHART 4-5
REGIONAL DEVIATIONS FROM U.S. AVERAGE IN THE
NUMBER OF SCIENTISTS AND ENGINEERS IN INDUSTRIAL
RESEARCH AND DEVELOPMENT PER 10,000 WORKERS IN
THE LABOR FORCE, 1966

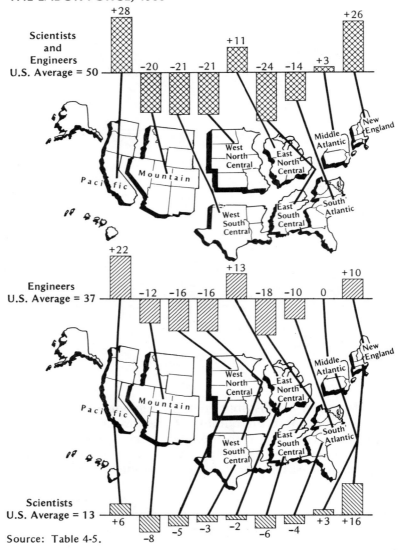

Source: Table 4-5.

82

Regional Patterns in Academic R&D Manpower

Table 4-6 and Chart 4-6 provide information on the number of full-time equivalent scientists and engineers employed in colleges and universities in teaching, R&D or other activities in 1974. The colleges and universities in the East North Central, South Atlantic and Middle Atlantic regions employ the largest absolute numbers of full-time equivalent scientists and engineers, about 40-50 thousand each. However, in terms of the number per million population, the New England region clearly stands out from the rest. Whereas the other regions employ about 1,200 per million population, the New England region employs over 1,800. Also, the scientists and engineers at New England colleges and universities do relatively more R&D work than those in the other regions.

TABLE 4-6

PERCENTAGES OF TIME SPENT BY ACADEMIC SCIENTISTS AND ENGINEERS
IN TEACHING, R&D WORK AND IN OTHER EFFORTS, UNITED STATES, 1974

Census Regions	Full-time Equivalents			
	Total	Research & Development	Teaching	Other
United States	100%	18%	76%	6%
New England	100	24	73	3
Middle Atlantic	100	15	81	4
East North Central	100	15	76	9
West North Central	100	17	76	7
South Atlantic	100	18	76	6
East South Central	100	13	78	9
West South Central	100	16	70	14
Mountain	100	18	75	7
Pacific	100	21	76	3

Sources: National Science Foundation, "Manpower Resources for Scientific Activities at Universities and Colleges, January 1974," Detailed Statistical Tables, Appendix B, NSF 75-300-A (Washington, D.C.: National Science Foundation, December 1974), Table B-28, p. 28; U.S. Bureau of the Census, "Population Profile of the United States: 1974," Current Population Reports, p-20, No. 279 (Washington, D.C.: U.S. Government Printing Office, March 1975), Table 17, p. 23.

CHART 4-6
FULL-TIME EQUIVALENT SCIENTISTS AND ENGINEERS EMPLOYED IN COLLEGES AND UNIVERSITIES IN TEACHING, R&D AND OTHER ACTIVITIES, BY CENSUS REGION, 1974

Number in Thousands

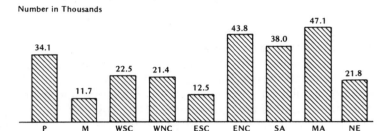

Number per Million Population

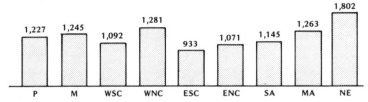

Percentage Distribution of Time by Activity

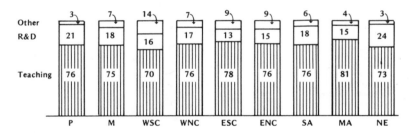

Source: See Table 4-6.

Notes

1 U.S. Department of Labor, Bureau of Labor Statistics, *Scientific and Technical Personnel in Industry, 1969,* Bulletin 1723 (Washington, D.C.: U.S. Government Printing Office, 1971), Table 12, p. 34.

Part III

INDICATORS OF THE ECONOMIC AND SOCIAL IMPACT OF SCIENCE AND RESEARCH

5   The Diffusion of Eight Major Industrial Innovations in the United States

Edwin Mansfield

Introduction

The rate of diffusion of new technology is of great importance since new techniques can have little or no impact on productivity and living standards unless they are applied. In recent years, there has been some research by economists directed at measuring the rates of diffusion of new techniques and at explaining observed differences among innovations, industries and nations in the rates of diffusion. These studies have been carried out by (among others) Griliches, Nabseth and Ray, Romeo, and myself.[1] The results, although subject to obvious limitations, seem to have shed new light on this important, and hitherto largely neglected, area.

My purpose here is to present data concerning the rate of diffusion in the United States of eight major innovations: numerically controlled machine tools; the basic oxygen process in steel making; catalytic cracking of petroleum; large-scale ammonia plants; acrylonitrile from propylene; the oxychlorination process for vinyl chloride; discrete semiconductors; and nuclear power. The extent of the savings from each of these innovations will also be explored. Where possible, the data have been taken from secondary sources, but in some cases primary sources had to be utilized. The results, which are largely descriptive,[2] are meant to help the National Planning Association in its attempts "to develop quantitative indicators of the current and recent rates of diffusion of selected industrial innovations which have had appreciable effects on productivity. . . ."[3]

Numerically Controlled Machine Tools

Numerically controlled (NC) machine tools are operated by numerical instructions expressed in code. Prepared in advance and recorded on tapes or cards, these instructions control the sequence of machine operations. They determine the machine positions, the speed and direction of movement of the tool or workpiece and the flow of coolant. Numerical control results in a great many economic advantages. 1. There is the virtual elimination of templates, jigs and fixtures. Simple, virtually universal work-holding devices can be used, the result being lower tooling costs, faster setup time, shorter lead time and decreased tooling storage space. 2. Numerical control allows lot sizes to be tailored more closely to actual requirements, and makes possible a reduction in inventories. 3. Machining time and floor space are generally reduced by numerical control. 4. Numerical control results in greater accuracy and uniformity, and makes possible the machining of formerly "impossible" jobs.

In 1955, the first commercial NC machine tools were shown at the National Machine Tool Show. The research and development underlying this innovation seems to have begun in 1947, when John T. Parsons received a study contract from the air force. Parsons, owner of a small Michigan firm that produced rotor blades, had conceived a jig borer that was coupled with automatic data processing equipment. After receiving the contract, Parsons turned for help to MIT's Servomechanism Laboratory, which subsequently was given a direct contract for the development of an experimental milling machine. By late 1952, MIT had successfully developed the first such machine. Various refinements were then made by machine tool builders and makers of control and computer equipment, as well as by MIT.

In general, numerically controlled machine tools have proved quite profitable to American industry. According to a 1970 survey of about 80 firms, the average payout period for investment in the first NC machine tool (for the firms in the survey) in each industry was: aircraft engines, 2.2 years; airframes, 3.2 years; printing presses, 5.8 years; coal mining machinery, 4.0 years; digital computers, 2.2 years; large steam turbines, 4.0 years; machine tools, 3.4 years; farm machinery, 4.3 years; tools and dies, 5.1 years; and industrial instruments, 3.1 years.[4] In the tool and die industry, a survey of about 100 firms was carried out in 1968, the results indicating that the payout period was 3 years or less in about one-third of the cases and 5 years or less in about two-thirds of the cases. For 12 of the firms, a detailed study was made of the savings due to numerical control.[5] See Appendix

Table 5-1 for these results.

However, it should not be assumed that NC machine tools can be used profitably for all types of work. An important factor determining the profitability of using numerical control is the lot size: conventional machine tools can often produce single items or very small lot sizes at lower cost than NC machine tools. Also, when the lot size is very large, conventional tools are cheaper than NC tools. Thus, NC machine tools are more economical when the lot size is intermediate.

There are at least two principal ways to measure the rate of diffusion of a new type of equipment. One way is to measure the increase over time in the percent of *output* or *capacity* that is accounted for by the innovation. A second way is to measure the increase over time in the percent of *purchases* of equipment that are of the new type. Obviously, these two methods are designed to measure quite different things. In the case of all other innovations taken up in this chapter, the emphasis will be on the first type of measure. But in this case, the second measure is emphasized because of data limitations. Only rather sketchy data are available concerning the percentage of the stock of U.S. machine tools that are numerically controlled. According to rough estimates made by Gebhardt and Hatzold, there were about 12,000 NC machine tools in the United States in 1967, 18,000 in 1969 and 20,000 in 1970.[6]

Based on data collected by the Department of Commerce, we can calculate the percentage of value of shipments of metal-cutting machine tools that were numerically controlled for each year since 1959. The results, shown in Chart 5-1, indicate that this percentage grew from almost 4 percent in 1959 to 13 percent in 1963 to 27 percent in 1968. In 1970, this percentage fell to 19 percent, probably due to the recession. During 1971-74, it has remained between 20 and 25 percent. According to Department of Commerce experts, one factor responsible for the recent stability of this percentage has been decreases in the price of NC machine tools. Table 5-1 shows that the rate of diffusion has varied from industry to industry. According to Romeo's results, the rate of diffusion has tended to be higher in industries where NC machine tools were more profitable, where the ratio of R&D expenditures to sales was high, and where concentration was low.

CHART 5-1

VALUE OF SHIPMENTS OF NC MACHINE TOOLS AS A PERCENT
OF VALUE OF SHIPMENTS OF ALL METAL-CUTTING MACHINE
TOOLS, 1959-74

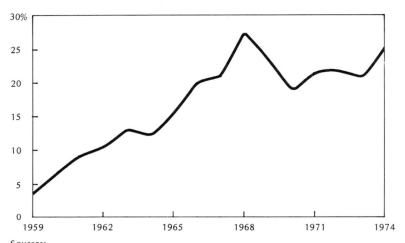

Sources:
E. Schwartz and T. Prenting, "Automation in the Fabricating Industries," in
*Report of the National Commission on Technology, Automation, and Economic
Progress*, Vol. I, 1966, p. 316; and *Current Industrial Reports*, U.S. Department
of Commerce, 1966–74. For data see Appendix Table 5-2.

The Basic Oxygen Steel Process

After World War II, engineers at the Linz steel complex in Austria
began a series of experiments concerning the use of oxygen in
steel production. The basic idea behind these experiments dates
back to Henry Bessemer's work in the mid-19th century. But,
because low-cost oxygen was not available (and for other reasons), this idea was not applied widely until after World War II.
After a series of unsuccessful attempts, the Austrian engineers
were able in 1949 to produce good quality steel without damag-
ing the vessel or destroying the lance. In 1952, they went from a 2-
ton vessel to a 35-ton vessel, and in 1953 established a second
plant at Donawitz. From Linz-Donawitz, the procedure acquired
its name—the LD process. After the advent of the 35-ton oxygen
converter, numerous improvements and extensions were carried out, particularly to widen the product mix and to make the
process suitable for high phosphorus ores.

TABLE 5-1

APPROXIMATE NUMBER OF YEARS FROM FIRST ADOPTION TO DATE
WHEN 25 PERCENT OF INDUSTRY'S NEW MACHINE TOOL PURCHASES
WERE NUMERICALLY CONTROLLED, 10 INDUSTRIES

Industry	Number of Years
Aircraft engines	13
Airframes	13
Printing presses	12
Coal mining machinery	10
Digital computers	9
Large steam turbines	9
Machine tools	9
Farm machinery	15
Tool and die	13
Industrial instruments	6

Source: A. Romeo, "Interindustry and Interfirm Differences in the Rate of
Diffusion of an Innovation," Review of Economics and Statistics, August
1975.

The LD oxygen converter must be charged with hot metal, and
thus must be near a blast furnace. Scrap is charged first, after
which the molten ore is poured in. The vessel is then put back in
an upright position, and the lance is lowered until it is 4-8 feet
above the metal. The lance, a tube about 50 feet long and 10
inches in diameter, is water cooled to withstand the furnace heat.
It injects oxygen of 99.5 percent purity, the resulting oxidation
burning part of the iron and nearly all of the carbon, manganese,
phosphorus and silicon impurities. When the carbon is gone, the
fire burns out. Oxygen converters must have a charge made up of
70-75 percent or more of hot metal, which means that a maxi-
mum of 30 percent can be scrap. This is in contrast to the present
practice of using 50 percent scrap in open-hearth furnaces and
up to 90 percent in electric furnaces.

The oxygen process is frequently, but not always, cheaper than
open-hearth or electric furnaces. An important point in its favor
is that the capital cost of an oxygen converter is only about one-
half of the capital cost of an open hearth. However, if a blast
furnace is not already nearby, this cost advantage may be offset.
(Moreover, the capital cost of an electric furnace can, under
some circumstances, be lower than either oxygen converters or

open hearths.) Nonetheless, the lower capital cost of the oxygen process has been an important factor in its displacement of the open hearth. For example, in 1957, it was estimated that the capital cost of the basic oxygen process was about $15 per ton, as compared with about $40 per ton for an open hearth.

Another factor that will increase the profitability of the oxygen process is an increase in the price of scrap. As noted above, oxygen converters use less scrap than do open hearths. Thus, a higher relative price of scrap will raise the cost of production of open hearths relative to that of oxygen converters. According to Meyer and Herregat, with low scrap prices, electric furnaces may have lower production costs than oxygen converters, if the scale of operations is small. But, if the scale is large, oxygen converters seem to have lower costs than open hearths or electric furnaces, even if scrap prices are relatively low.[7]

It is difficult to get reliable or meaningful figures comparing the costs of production of various steel processes. According to data presented in a study done for the Economic Commission of Latin America, the total cost of producing 1.5 million tons of ingot per year was about 11 percent lower for the basic oxygen process than for an open hearth in 1962. Although this comparison is of interest, it must be borne in mind that a host of factors, some of which were cited above, will influence the relative costs of these processes in a particular situation.[8]

To measure the rate of diffusion of the basic oxygen process in the United States, we calculated the percentage of American steel output produced each year by the basic oxygen process. The data underlying these computations were obtained from the American Iron and Steel Institute. The results, shown in Chart 5-2, indicate that the oxygen process produced less than 5 percent of U.S. steel up until 1962, about 25 percent in 1966, about 37 percent in 1968, and about 56 percent in 1974. Clearly, the oxygen process has steadily displaced other steelmaking techniques in the United States. Whether this diffusion process has occurred as rapidly as it should is a matter of controversy. According to some observers, Dirlam and Adams among others,[9] the American steel industry has been relatively slow to introduce the oxygen process; however, the steel producers have denied this charge.[10] Perhaps the most complete study has been carried out by Tsao and Day who, using a linear programming model, concluded that the diffusion rate was close to optimal.[11] Also, it is worth noting that Gold, Peirce and Rosegger found that, of 14 steel innovations, the oxygen process seemed to spread more rapidly than over half of the other processes.[12]

CHART 5-2
PERCENTAGE OF U.S. STEEL OUTPUT PRODUCED BY BASIC OXYGEN PROCESS, 1958-74

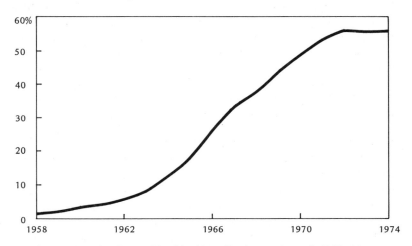

Source: American Iron and Steel Institute. For data see Appendix Table 5-2.

Catalytic Cracking of Petroleum

The basic invention of catalytic cracking was due primarily to Eugene Houdry, a French inventor who worked for many years on catalysis and its effect on cracking. In 1927, he successfully produced for the first time motor gasoline from a heavy petroleum fraction. After seeking financial support for subsequent stages of the project for a number of years, he convinced Sun Oil and Socony-Mobil to back his work. By 1936, a commercial installation was made, and catalytic cracking was a practical reality. However, numerous improvements were made in the original Houdry process. In particular, the Thermofor process (due to Socony-Mobil and Houdry) and the Houdriflow process (due to Houdry) made the cracking process continuous rather than semicontinuous, as was the case for the original Houdry process. The Thermofor process was first installed in 1944, the Houdriflow process in 1950.

91

With the exception of Socony-Mobil and Sun (stockholders with Eugene Houdry in the Houdry Process Corporation), all of the other oil firms were confronted with the choice of licensing the new process (and paying considerable royalties) or of trying to invent around Houdry's patents. A number of the major companies, including Standard Oil of New Jersey, Kellogg, Standard Oil of Indiana, British Petroleum, Shell, Texaco and UOP, pooled their resources in what was probably the biggest single development effort prior to the Manhattan Project in an attempt to invent around the patents. Led by Standard Oil of New Jersey (now Exxon), they spent about $30 million between 1935 and 1945 on development work, from which emerged a new catalytic process, Fluid Catalytic Cracking. An important feature of the new process was that it used a fluidized catalyst bed. The first commercial introduction of this new process took place in 1942.

Catalytic cracking resulted in a marked reduction in the cost of transportation. According to John Enos, the Houdry process resulted in about a 70 percent decrease in fuel inputs (per 100,000 ton-miles of transportation) relative to the Tube and Tank process that preceded it. However, there was no saving in labor, raw material or capital. The Fluid Catalytic Cracking process resulted in further savings. Specifically, it reduced labor inputs by about 90 percent, raw material inputs by about 50 percent, fuel inputs by about 20 percent, and capital inputs by about 10 percent relative to the original Houdry process. Thus, catalytic cracking meant very substantial productivity gains to the oil industry.[13]

From the point of view of the inventors and innovators, catalytic cracking was also a very profitable venture. Eugene Houdry and his associates invested about $3 million in the invention, and got back about $13 million. The Houdry Process Corporation invested about $11 million in the innovation, and got back about $39 million. Figures regarding the profitability of Fluid Catalytic Cracking are much less precise, but it appears that it also was a very profitable undertaking.

To measure the rate of diffusion of catalytic cracking, we used the growth over time in the percentage of total U.S. cracking capacity that was catalytic. Chart 5-3 shows that by 1940, catalytic cracking accounted for about 5 percent of the total, and that the percentage grew to about 10 percent in 1943, about 30 percent in 1946, about 50 percent in 1952, and about 80 percent in 1956. These figures were obtained from the Annual Refining issues of the *Oil and Gas Journal*. Included in these figures are shutdown plants. Thus, if a disproportionate percentage of the shutdown plants are thermal, these figures may underestimate somewhat the rate of diffusion.

CHART 5-3
CATALYTIC CRACKING CAPACITY AS A PERCENT OF
TOTAL U.S. CRACKING CAPACITY, 1937-75

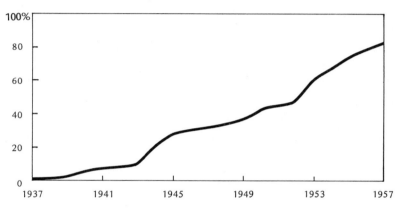

Source: *Oil and Gas Journal.* For data see Appendix Table 5-2.

It was also possible to obtain data (from the same source) concerning the diffusion of individual types of catalytic cracking processes. As shown in Table 5-2 the Houdry process reached about 9 percent of total cracking capacity in 1944 and then slowly declined. The Thermofor process reached about 6 percent in 1945 and grew steadily to about 16 percent in 1956. The Fluid Catalytic Cracking process quickly gained the lion's share of the nation's capacity; it jumped from 2 percent in 1943 to 17 percent in 1947 to 31 percent in 1952 and to 62 percent in 1957. The Houdriflow process did not account for more than 4 percent of total capacity.

Large-Scale Ammonia Plants

In 1965, Monsanto put into operation the first large-scale syn-

TABLE 5-2

PERCENT OF TOTAL U.S. CRACKING CAPACITY ACCOUNTED FOR BY
EACH TYPE OF CATALYTIC PROCESS

Year	Houdry	Houdriflow	Thermofor	Fluid
1937	0.1	-	-	-
1938	0.6	-	-	-
1939	1.1	-	-	-
1940	5.6	-	-	-
1941	6.6	-	-	-
1942	7.0	-	-	-
1943	7.9	-	-	2.0
1944	9.2	-	3.0	9.2
1945	8.4	-	6.5	13.3
1946	8.7	-	6.9	14.1
1947	8.0	-	6.9	16.8
1948	7.4	-	7.1	18.9
1949	6.9	-	7.9	22.2
1950	6.0	0.5	7.5	27.7
1951	5.7	1.3	8.5	28.3
1952	5.1	1.8	8.7	31.0
1953	4.0	2.3	12.4	42.1
1954	3.9	2.5	13.9	46.8
1955	3.3	2.9	15.5	52.7
1956	1.2	4.0	16.0	57.6
1957	0.9	3.8	15.2	61.6

Source: Oil and Gas Journal.

thetic ammonia plant. Designed by M. W. Kellogg, this plant used relatively inexpensive, small centrifugal compressors to reduce the operating pressure, when combining free hydrogen and nitrogen gas into anhydrous ammonia, to about half the conventional pressure. Of course, centrifugal compressors were not new, but their use in ammonia production was an important innovation which cut costs considerably in large plants. To be economical, it has been estimated that a plant must have a capacity of 500 tons per day. The original Monsanto plant had a capacity of 600 tons per day, and many recent plants have capacities of 1,400 tons per day or more.

According to one report, a 1,000-ton-per-day plant of this new type can reduce operating costs by as much as 50 percent relative to previous standards. One reason for the lower costs is that labor input is reduced considerably. For example, Olin Mathieson reported that it employed 32 people (13 operators, 8 loaders and 11 supervisors, technicians and secretaries) at its Lake Charles plant, a 1,400-ton-per-day plant built along the new lines in 1965. This contrasted with 71 people employed at its older plant, which had only one-fourth the capacity of the newer one.[14] Because of lower labor and maintenance costs (among other things), firms often replaced existing smaller ammonia plants with large plants of the newer type. According to the Stanford Research Institute, investment costs per ton of output are also lower with the big plants, the result being that manufacturing costs in 1969 were as low as $15-17 per short ton of ammonia (based on 1,000 tons per day and natural gas at 20 cents per mcf).[15] Costs with older types of plants at that time are shown in Appendix Chart 5-1.

During the 1960s, U.S. ammonia capacity grew at an enormous rate. In 1960, total capacity was about 5 million short tons per year; in 1965, it was almost 9 million short tons per year; and in 1970, it was about 17 million short tons per year. This increase in capacity was due largely to increases in the demand for fertilizer, both here and abroad. Since 1970, there has been little increase in total ammonia capacity in the United States. Practically all of the new capacity introduced since 1965 has been based on the new technology embodied in large-scale plants.

To measure the rate of diffusion of large-scale ammonia plants, we calculated the growth over time in the percentage of U.S. ammonia capacity that is accounted for by plants of 600 tons per day or more. The Stanford Research Institute published data that were used to calculate these percentages.[16] The results, shown in Chart 5-4, indicate that large-scale plants accounted for about 6 percent of total capacity in 1966, about 40 percent in 1968, about 60 percent in 1970 and about 80 percent in 1974. Clearly, this innovation spread rapidly.

It is important to note that the capacity data used in Chart 5-4 are not entirely comparable over time. As the Stanford Research Institute points out, the figures for 1965-67 represent optimum capacity rather than rated capacity, whereas later figures represent rated capacity. Many of the new large plants cannot run effectively at their rated capacities. Also, the fact that some ammonia plants use interruptible gas means that their real capacity is somewhat lower than is indicated in Chart 5-4.

CHART 5-4

CAPACITY OF LARGE-SCALE AMMONIA PLANTS (600 TONS PER DAY OR MORE) AS PERCENT OF TOTAL U.S. AMMONIA CAPACITY, 1965-74

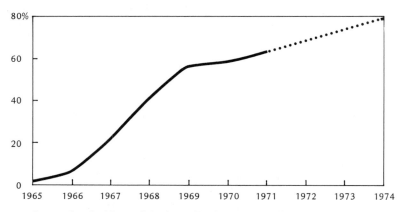

Source: Stanford Research Institute. For data see Appendix Table 5-2.

Acrylonitrile from Propylene

Acrylonitrile is the principal intermediate used in the production of acrylic fibers. In 1971, acrylic fibers formed 61 percent of its market, ABS and SAN resins formed 17 percent, and nitrile rubber formed 6 percent. In 1940, acrylonitrile was first commercialized by American Cyanamid to produce nitrile rubber. A number of other firms built acrylonitrile plants during World War II because nitrile rubber was used in the war effort. After the war, government demand for nitrile rubber receded, and all producers other than American Cyanamid closed their acrylonitrile plants. In 1952, with the increased demand for acrylic fibers, Monsanto and Union Carbide began producing acrylonitrile followed by Goodrich, DuPont and Sohio.

American Cyanamid and Union Carbide used ethylene oxide and hydrogen cyanide to produce acrylonitrile. Monsanto used a reaction of acetylene with hydrogen cyanide. Monsanto's process made the ethylene oxide process obsolete, and Cyanamid, Goodrich and DuPont built plants that used acetylene as a feedstock. By 1955, over half of the acrylonitrile in the United

States was produced from acetylene, not ethylene oxide. By 1960, only about one-fourth of the acrylonitrile was produced from ethylene oxide.

In 1960, Standard Oil of Ohio (Sohio) began using a process utilizing propylene and ammonia as feedstocks. This new process revolutionized the production of acrylonitrile, its costs being so low relative to the older process that all other producers eventually had to shut down their plants. With the exception of Union Carbide (which left the market completely in 1967), all the other producers licensed the new process from Sohio and constructed new propylene-based plants. According to Peter Simon, the typical investment in the new plants paid back in about two and one-half years. However, he is careful to point out that his figures are very rough.[17]

To measure the rate of diffusion of the Sohio process for producing acrylonitrile, we calculated the growth over time in the percentage of acrylonitrile produced from propylene in the United States. These calculations were based on data obtained from the Stanford Research Institute.[18] The results, shown in Chart 5-5, indicated that the rate of diffusion was very rapid. In 1961, about one-tenth of all acrylonitrile was produced from propylene; in 1964, about one-third was produced from propylene; in 1969, about nine-tenths was produced from propylene; and in 1971, the new process had completely displaced the old.

Oxychlorination Process for Vinyl Chloride

Vinyl chloride is the monomer that is used to make polyvinyl chloride. Polyvinyl chloride (PVC) is one of the most important plastics, much of it being used for flooring and packaging, cable insulations, rainwear, shoe soles, piping and building components. Although polyvinyl chloride has been known for over a century, it was first produced commercially by I.G. Farben in the 1930s. Flexible polyvinyl chloride accounted for the bulk of its uses for many years, but rigid forms of PVC, introduced in the 1950s, have become important as well. In 1964, when the oxychlorination process for vinyl chloride was first used, the value of PVC production in the United States was $277 million.

CHART 5-5

PERCENT OF ACRYLONITRILE PRODUCED FROM PROPYLENE,
UNITED STATES, 1960-71

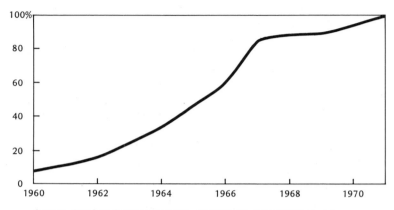

Source: Stanford Research Institute. For data see Appendix Table 5-2.

Three methods have been used to make vinyl chloride in the United States. The earliest method, and the most widely used until the advent of oxychlorination, was the combination of acetylene with hydrochloric acid. The earliest plants of this type used carbide-derived acetylene and hydrochloric acid obtained by combusting hydrogen with chlorine. Gradually, carbide acetylene and purposely made hydrochloric acid were displaced by cheaper petroleum-based acetylene and the byproduct hydrochloric acid. Nonetheless, raw material costs were high relative to newer processes.

In the late 1940s, the second large-scale industrial process for the production of vinyl chloride was introduced. The ethylene dichloride process added chlorine to ethylene to produce ethylene dichloride, and then split off hydrochloric acid to produce vinyl chloride. In some cases, this process was used without an acetylene unit. Ethyl used this process and employed the byproduct hydrochloric acid to make ethyl chloride for use in the manufacture of tetraethyl lead compounds. Generally, however, since firms could not justify sufficient use of the byproduct hydrochloric acid, a balanced ethylene-acetylene complex resulted, with the excess hydrochloric acid being used to make vinyl chloride directly.[19]

In 1964, the oxychlorination process for the production of vinyl chloride was first introduced. This process, developed by B.G. Goodrich, prevents the accumulation of a large hydrochloric acid byproduct, as well as the need for acetylene feedstock. The oxychlorination process resulted in considerable savings over the older processes. As shown in Chart 5-6, the capital cost per unit of capacity is higher for oxychlorination than for the balanced acetylene-ethylene process. But the reduction in raw material costs has been big enough to offset this disadvantage. For example, at ethylene and acetylene prices of 3 and 8 cents per pound, the change in feedstocks reduced raw material costs by about 1.1 cents per pound, according to Keane, Stobaugh and Townsend.[20] Thus, the material saving for a 500-million-pound-per-year plant was about $5 million annually, which certainly offset the $3 to $4 million increase in capital costs. Indeed, the older processes simply could not compete, except in special circumstances, with oxychlorination.

CHART 5-6
ESTIMATED CAPITAL COST FOR ALTERNATIVE PROCESSES FOR VINYL CHLORIDE

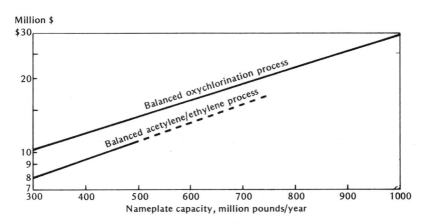

Source: P. Spitz, "Vinyl Chloride Economics," *Chemical Engineering Progress* (March 1968); and D. Keane, R. Stobaugh and P. Townsend, "Vinyl Chloride," *Hydrocarbon Processing* (February 1973).

To measure the rate of diffusion of the oxychlorination process, we calculated the growth over time in the percentage of U.S.

vinyl chloride capacity that used the oxychlorination process. Using data published periodically in the *Oil, Paint, and Drug Reporter,* as well as by Stobaugh and his colleagues, it was possible to make these calculations. The results, shown in Chart 5-7, indicate that the oxychlorination process spread quickly. By 1966, about 40 percent of the vinyl chloride capacity utilized oxychlorination; by 1969, the percentage was about 70; and by 1972, it was over 80.[21]

CHART 5-7
PERCENT OF VINYL CHLORIDE PRODUCED BY OXYCHLORI-NATION PROCESS, UNITED STATES, 1965-72

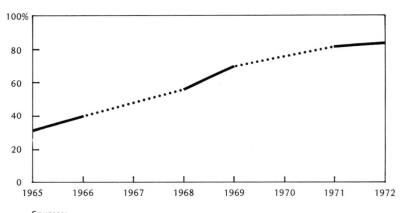

Sources:
Oil, Paint, and Drug Reporter, October 18, 1965, April 29, 1968, March 17, 1969, October 11, 1971; R. Stobaugh, *Petrochemical Manufacturing and Marketing Guide,* Gulf, 1968; and D. Keane, R. Stobaugh and P. Townsend, "Vinyl Chloride," *Hydrocarbon Processing,* February 1973. For data see Appendix Table 5-2.

Discrete Semiconductors

In 1948, the Bell Telephone Laboratories made known the invention of the point contact transistor; three years later, it announced the invention of the junction transistor. These inventions were among the most important of recent times; the three principal inventors, William Shockley, John Bardeen and Walter Brattain, received a Nobel Prize in 1956. The transistor is one type of discrete semiconductor; diodes (including rectifiers) and

100

special devices are others. Although transistors and diodes do different things, their production is rather similar, and most transistor producers also make diodes.

With improvements in the production technology underlying discrete semiconductors, there was a remarkable reduction in cost and increase in reliability and frequency during the 1950s and early 1960s. The result was a substantial increase in the potential market for discrete semiconductors. When the transistor first appeared, it was costly relative to the receiving tube, and was used only where its small size, low power consumption and other special features were of great importance. For example, one of the first areas where transistors were substituted for receiving tubes was in hearing aids. But as its price fell and its performance improved, the transistor was substituted for tubes in computers, radios, television sets, tape recorders and many other products. Moreover, with improvements in diodes and special devices, they too have found wider markets.

It is important to recognize that discrete semiconductors did more than simply replace the receiving tube. They opened up entirely new areas, not feasible previously because of the tube's technological limitations. Among the most important of these limitations were the inefficiency, low reliability, size and fragility of tubes. Because discrete semiconductors did not have these limitations, they enabled producers to make entirely new types of equipment, such as very small computers. These new capabilities were important in military as well as purely commercial fields.[22]

To measure the rate of diffusion of discrete semiconductors in the United States, we calculated the growth over time in the value of output of discrete semiconductors as a percent of the value of output of receiving tubes plus discrete semiconductors. On the basis of data published by the Business and Defense Services Administration and the Electronic Industries Association, it was possible to carry out these calculations. The results, shown in Chart 5-8, indicate that discrete semiconductors reached about 10 percent of the total value of output in1955, about 30 percent in 1957, about 60 percent in 1960 and about 80 percent in 1966. Clearly, the rate of diffusion was relatively rapid.

CHART 5-8

VALUE OF OUTPUT OF DISCRETE SEMICONDUCTORS AS A PERCENT OF VALUE OF OUTPUT OF DISCRETE SEMICONDUCTORS AND RECEIVING TUBES, UNITED STATES, 1952-68

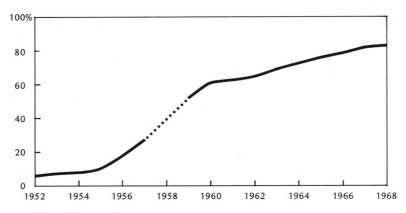

Sources:
Business and Defense Services Administration; and J. Tilton, *International Diffusion of Technology: The Case of Semiconductors* (Brookings, 1971). For data see Appendix Table 5-2.

Two points should be made concerning the data in Chart 5-8. First, there is no reason to believe that the percentage shown will eventually reach 100. Semiconductors were not superior substitutes for receiving tubes in all applications. Second, the increase in the percentage shown in the chart was due largely to the great increase in the value of output of semiconductors, not to a great decline in the value of output of receiving tubes. For example, the value of receiving tube output in 1968 was only about one-third less than its peak in 1957.

Finally, we followed Tilton in including the output of monolithic integrated circuits with the output of discrete semiconductors in Chart 5-8.[23] Since the output of integrated circuits during the early 1960s was small relative to that of discrete semiconductors, the results are not greatly affected by this procedure.

Nuclear Power

In 1938, Otto Hahn and Fritz Strassmann "discovered" nuclear fission in their studies of the substances obtained when neutrons impinge on the uranium nucleus. Their work, as well as that of Fermi, Bohr, Wheeler and others, formed the basis for nuclear reactors. A nuclear reactor produces electricity by producing heat. Generally, a reactor will contain fissionable material, control rods, a moderator, shielding, and structural materials and mechanisms for removing the heat that is generated. The capital cost of a nuclear power reactor tends to be high because of the complexity of the plant.

Atomic energy came into being for military purposes during World War II, and, for some time, private industry in the United States was prohibited from developing nuclear power. Then the AEC Act of 1954 permitted private industry to own and operate nuclear reactors, but the ownership of nuclear fuels (and certain important elements of nuclear technology) resided with the government. In 1964, the AEC Act was amended to allow private ownership of nuclear fuels. The first commercial nuclear power plant in the United States was Duquesne Light's Shippingport plant, which began operation in 1957.

For a variety of reasons, nuclear power has become controversial in the United States. For one thing, there has been considerable discussion of possible dangers to the environment and to public safety. As critics of nuclear power point out, reactors release a certain amount of irradiated wastes, the disposal of nuclear wastes can cause problems, and thermal pollution can pose an environmental threat. Further, there are possible dangers associated with the use of fissionable materials to make bombs and with the sabotage of nuclear power plants by terrorists. Although the probability of some of these disastrous events unquestionably is low, some citizens regard it as too high to be acceptable. Others feel that nuclear reactors are a relatively safe and important part of our nation's energy future.[24]

In addition, there has been considerable controversy over the costs (narrowly defined) of nuclear power and of conventional power. Many advocates of nuclear power have insisted that it is competitive (or that it soon would be) with conventional power. Critics, on the other hand, have claimed that this is not true. For example, Philip Sporn estimated in 1970 that the cost of switchboard-delivered nuclear power was 7.06 mills per kilowatt-hour as against 6.65 mills for coal-fired energy with coal at 25 cents per million BTU. Of course, as the Office of Science and Technology pointed out in its comments on Sporn's report, this is a field where change, both economic and technological, is rapid, and where such comparisons can become obsolete quickly.[25]

To measure the rate of diffusion of nuclear power in the United States, we calculated the growth over time in the percent of installed electrical generating capacity that is nuclear. Based on data published by the Federal Power Commission, it was possible to make these calculations for 1959 to 1974. The results, shown in Chart 5-9, indicate that the diffusion process has gone on more slowly than for the other innovations in this study. By 1974, less than 7 percent of all U.S. electrical generating capacity was nuclear. Chart 5-10, which contains the percentage of increased capacity that was nuclear, shows that this percentage increased considerably during the late 1960s and early 1970s. In 1967, 4 percent of new capacity was nuclear; by 1974, 28 percent was nuclear.

International Differences in Rates of Acceptance

Having described the rate of diffusion of each of these eight innovations in the United States, we will briefly discuss the international differences in their rates of acceptance. Data are presented only for numerically controlled machine tools, the basic oxygen process, semiconductors and nuclear power, since these are the innovations for which the data are most plentiful.

Numerically Controlled Machine Tools

On the basis of a survey carried out by Gebhardt and Hatzold, it appears that the rate of acceptance of NC machine tools was much faster in the United States than in Austria, Italy, Sweden, the United Kingdom or West Germany. Using data for the pump, turning machine, turbine and printing machine industries, they found that in 1960, 36 percent of the U.S. firms in the sample had begun using NC machine tools, whereas only 8 percent of the British firms and none of the firms in other countries had done so. By 1962, NC machine tools were being used by 82 percent of the U.S. firms, 42 percent of the West German firms, 20 percent of the British firms, 6 percent of the Swedish firms, and none of the Austrian or Italian firms in the sample. Of course, one factor

CHART 5-9

NUCLEAR CAPACITY AS A PERCENT OF ALL INSTALLED
ELECTRICAL GENERATING CAPACITY,
UNITED STATES, 1959-74

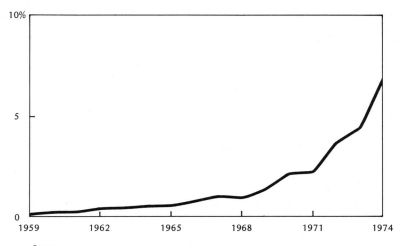

Sources:
Statistical Abstract of the United States; and the Federal Power Commission. For
data see Appendix Table 5-2.

responsible for the more rapid acceptance of NC machine tools
in the United States was the fact that they originated here.
Another factor, according to Gebhardt and Hatzold, was that
wage rates are higher in the United States than in the other
countries included in the sample.

The Basic Oxygen Process

Meyer and Herregat provide data concerning 11 countries for
the period 1956-59. As shown in Chart 5-11, the percentage of
total steel output produced by the oxygen process in 1969 was
highest in Austria, Japan and the Netherlands, and lowest in
France, the United Kingdom and Italy. Relative to this group of
countries, the U.S. percentage in 1969 was about in the middle.
Of course, one reason for the rapid rate of acceptance in Austria

CHART 5-10
INCREASE IN NUCLEAR ELECTRICAL CAPACITY AS A PERCENT
OF INCREASE IN ALL INSTALLED ELECTRICAL CAPACITY,
UNITED STATES, 1969-74

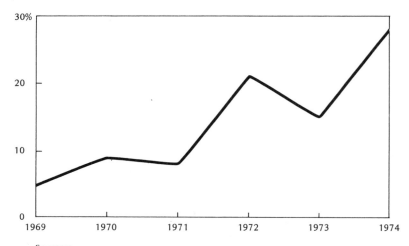

Sources:
Edison Electric Institute; and the Federal Power Commission. For data see Appendix Table 5-2.

was the fact that the process originated there. In Japan and the Netherlands, the relatively quick transition to the oxygen process was due in part to the fact that the Japanese and Dutch steel industries were expanding more rapidly than the steel industries in the other countries during this period. Thus, they could add oxygen converters to expand their capacity, whereas in the other countries, oxygen converters were more likely used to replace existing capacity.

Discrete Semiconductors

It is worth noting that the United States was generally the innovator in the area of discrete semiconductors. Table 5-3 shows the major innovations and the year when each was first produced in the United States, France, Germany, Great Britain and Japan. On the basis of these data, which were published by Tilton, we computed the average lag between the date of innovation and the time when each country began producing

CHART 5-11

SHARES OF BASIC OXYGEN STEEL IN TOTAL CRUDE STEEL OUTPUT

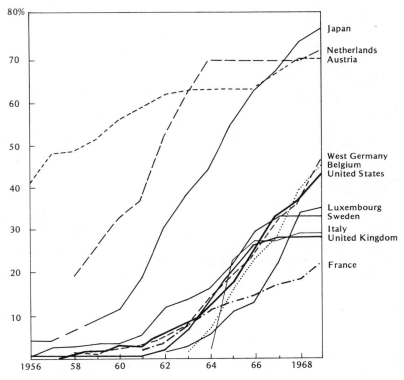

Source: L. Nabseth and F. Ray, *The Diffusion of New Technology* (New York and Cambridge: Cambridge University Press, 1974). Reprinted by permission of Cambridge University Press.

the innovation. The results indicate that the average lag was 0.1 years for the United States, 2.2 years for Great Britain, 2.5 years for Japan, 2.7 years for Germany, and 2.8 years for France. Clearly, the technology spread quickly from one nation to another.

It was also possible, on the basis of Tilton's data, to compare the rate of diffusion of discrete semiconductors in the United States with that in Japan and France. The results, shown in Chart 5-12, indicate that the time it took the United States to go from about 10 to 60 percent was roughly the same as the time it took France

TABLE 5-3

YEAR OF FIRST COMMERCIAL PRODUCTION OF MAJOR SEMICONDUCTOR
DEVICES, BY COUNTRY, 1951-68

Device	U.S.	U.K.	Japan	Germany	France
Point contact transistor	1951	1953	1953	1953	1952
Grown junction transistor	1951	--	1955	1953	1953
Alloy junction transistor	1952	1953	1954	1954	1954
Surface barrier transistor	1954	1958	1962	--	--
Silicon junction transistor	1954	1958	1959	1955	1960
Diffused transistor	1956	1959	1958	1959	1959
Silicon controlled rectifier	1956	1957	1960	1960	1960
Tunnel diode	1958	1960	1957	1960	1960
Planar transistor	1960	1961	1961	1962	1963
Epitaxial transistor	1960	1962	1961	1962	1963
Integrated circuit	1961	1962	1962	1965	1964
MOS transistor	1962	1964	1963	1965	1964
Gunn diode	1963	1965	1965	1967	1965

Source: J. Tilton, International Diffusion of Technology: The Case of Semiconductors
(Washington, D.C.: The Brookings Institution, 1971).

or Japan. However, the United States reached both the 10
percent mark and the 60 percent mark a year or two before
France or Japan. This, of course, would be expected, given the
fact (as noted previously) that semiconductor innovations generally originated in the United States.

Nuclear Power

Based on OECD data, the United Kingdom, France and Belgium
were accepting nuclear power much more rapidly than was the
United States during 1964-67. In each of these countries, 16-20
percent of new capacity was nuclear, as contrasted with about 3
percent in the United States. Italy was accepting it somewhat
more rapidly than was the United States, but Germany and
Sweden were not accepting it as rapidly as was the United States
during this period. In each of these countries (Italy, Germany and
Sweden), about 1-5 percent of new capacity was nuclear during
this period.[26] As of 1975, according to information provided by
the Energy Research and Development Administration, nuclear
energy accounted for a higher percentage of total electrical
capacity in the United Kingdom than in the United States. In
France, Switzerland and Germany, the percentage was about the
same as in the United States, whereas in Italy and Japan it was
lower.

CHART 5-12
VALUE OF SEMICONDUCTOR OUTPUT AS A PERCENTAGE OF
VALUE OF RECEIVING TUBE AND SEMICONDUCTOR
OUTPUT, 1952-68

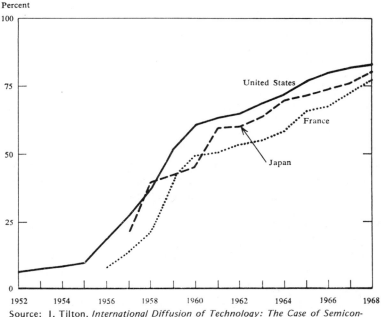

Source: J. Tilton, *International Diffusion of Technology: The Case of Semiconductors* (Washington, D.C.: © The Brookings Institution, 1971). Reprinted by permission of the Brookings Institution.

Variation Among Innovations and Over Time in Rates of Diffusion

Having described the rate of diffusion of each of the innovations in the United States, we will now compare the results for various innovations. As a crude measure of an innovation's rate of diffusion, we used the number of years that elapsed between the date an innovation was first introduced and the date it accounted for 50 percent of the relevant capacity or value of output. Table 5-4 shows this measure of the rate of diffusion for all of the innovations other than numerically controlled machine tools. (As pointed out in the section on NC machine tools, available data will not permit the computation of such a measure.) The results indicate substantial differences among these innovations in the rates of diffusion. In particular, large-scale ammonia

TABLE 5-4

NUMBER OF YEARS FROM FIRST INTRODUCTION TO DATE WHEN
50% OF OUTPUT (OR CAPACITY) WAS ACCOUNTED FOR BY THE
INNOVATION

Innovation	Number of Years
Basic oxygen process	17
Catalytic cracking	17
Large-scale ammonia plants	4
Acrylonitrile from propylene	6
Oxychlorination process for vinyl chloride	4
Discrete semiconductors	8
Nuclear power	>20

plants, the oxychlorination process and acrylonitrile from propylene showed rapid rates of diffusion relative to nuclear power, the basic oxygen process and catalytic cracking.

The reasons for the relatively slow diffusion of nuclear power have been cited above. Given the many questions that have been raised and the uncertainties expressed about the costs, both social and private, of nuclear power, it is understandable that its diffusion should have been relatively slow. Needless to say, this slow rate of diffusion need not be irrational or uneconomic. Under circumstances where there is great uncertainty concerning the social (and private) rate of return from the introduction of a new technology, the optimal strategy, both socially and privately, may be to proceed gradually, and to learn more about its effects and performance before making a more massive commitment to the innovation. The underlying question is whether the uncertainties are really as great as the critics of nuclear power claim them to be. Clearly, this question, which obviously cannot be treated, let alone answered, here, is of key importance in determining whether the rate of diffusion of nuclear power has been too slow.

Turning to the basic oxygen process and catalytic cracking, one reason why these innovations had relatively low rates of diffusion may have been that they were less profitable to adopt than were the others. According to Enos, an early adopter of catalytic cracking would have received about a 26 percent return on his investment[27] (as contrasted with Simon's estimate than an adopter of the oxychlorination process or the propylene route to acrylonitrile would have received a 40-50 percent return). According to Meyer and Herregat, it was not until the early 1960s that the steel industry could be sure that high carbon, silicon and alloy steels could be made in oxygen converters; [28] and, according to Dilley and McBride, investment in the oxygen process was not very profitable under American conditions in the early 1960s. [29] (However, as noted in the section on oxygen steel, this is a matter of controversy.) Another factor that may help to account for the observed differences in the rates of diffusion is the difference among industries in the amount spent on research and development. For a variety of reasons, one might expect that industries that spend more on R&D (as a percent of sales) would be quicker to adopt new technology. The innovations that spread most rapidly occurred in the chemical and electronics industries, both heavy spenders on R&D. The innovations that spread least rapidly occurred in the steel, electric power and petroleum industries, less research-intensive than the chemical or electronics industries. Of course, the observed correlation is hardly a test of this proposition. Moreover, there may well be more basic factors that influence both the rate of R&D spending and the rate of diffusion. However, it is worth noting (as was pointed out in the secton on NC machine tools), that differences among industries in the ratio of R&D expenditures to sales seem to be associated (in a statistically significant way) with differences in the rate of diffusion of numerically controlled machine tools.

Besides looking at differences among innovations in the rate of diffusion, it is also worthwhile to look at differences over time in the rate of diffusion. In other words, holding other relevant factors constant, does it appear that innovations spread more rapidly, or less rapidly, than in the past? Taken by itself our sample of eight innovations is obviously too small to shed much light on this subject. But if we compare the rate of diffusion of some of these innovations with that of earlier innovations in the same industry, the results may be of interest. Such a comparison can be made for two industries, steel and chemicals.

In the case of steel, we can compare the rate of diffusion of the basic oxygen process with that of earlier innovations, as measured by Gold, Peirce and Rosegger. [30] The results seem to indicate that the rate of diffusion is somewhat higher than in the past.

In the case of chemicals, a much more sophisticated (but still far from definitive) comparison can be made of the three chemical innovations discussed here—large-scale ammonia plants, acrylonitrile from propylene and the oxychlorination process—with 21 other innovations, based on Simon's work.[31] His data indicate that an innovation's rate of diffusion is affected by the profitability of the innovation to users and by whether or not the firms that imitated the innovator used its process or invented around it. Holding both of these variables constant, there is a tendency for the rate of diffusion to be higher for more recent innovations. Moreover, this tendency is statistically significant.

Summary and Conclusion

The diffusion of new technology is a vital part of the process that leads from the development of new processes and products to higher productivity and improved living standards. Here, we have been concerned almost entirely with the diffusion in the United States of eight major industrial innovations: numerically controlled machine tools, the basic oxygen process in steel, catalytic cracking of petroleum, large-scale ammonia plants, acrylonitrile from propylene, the oxychlorination process for vinyl chloride, discrete semiconductors, and nuclear power. With the exception of catalytic cracking, all of these innovations occurred after World War II. Four (NC machine tools, the oxygen process, semiconductors, and nuclear power) occurred in the 1950s, whereas three (large-scale ammonia plants, acrylonitrile from propylene and the oxychlorination process) occurred in the 1960s.

Our results indicate that there have been substantial differences in the rate of diffusion of these innovations. Because of public fears concerning possible hazards, as well as uncertainties concerning economic factors, nuclear power has spread much more slowly than the other innovations. In contrast, large-scale ammonia plants, the oxychlorination process, acrylonitrile from propylene, and discrete semiconductors accounted for half of the relevant capacity or output in four to eight years after their initial introduction, a relatively short period of time. The basic oxygen process and catalytic cracking had significantly lower diffusion rates, perhaps because, during the relevant period, they seem to have been less profitable to adopt than the innovations that spread more rapidly.

If these diffusion data are viewed as scientific or technological indicators, an important question is: Do they provide any indication that the American economy is slower to accept new technology than in the past? Obviously, this small-scale study of eight innovations can provide only a limited amount of evidence on this score. But what evidence it does provide (based on comparisons with earlier innovations) points in the opposite direction. In other words, a comparison of these innovations with earlier innovations in the same industries (where this is feasible) seems to indicate that, all other things being equal, these innovations tended to spread more rapidly than earlier innovations. Although this is an interesting finding, it is hardly unambiguous.

Because the diffusion process is characterized by varying degrees of uncertainty, because learning occurs on the part of producers and users of the innovation during this process, because the innovation itself may vary during this process, and because older techniques have the economic advantages associated with already being in place, it is extremely difficult to determine the socially optimal rate of diffusion of an innovation. Certainly, it would be naive to believe that the faster the diffusion rate, the better. No model presently exists that can be used to tell with confidence whether a certain diffusion rate was too high or too low. To make such a judgment, one would have to have far more information concerning technological and economic factors (and expectations) at various points in time than can generally be obtained.

Finally, in those cases where it is possible to compare an innovation's rate of acceptance in the United States with that in other countries, the results vary considerably from innovation to innovation. With regard to NC machine tools and semiconductors, the U.S. rate of acceptance seemed at least as high as that in any other country for which we have data. However, for the basic oxygen process and nuclear power, the U.S. rate of acceptance was lower than that of other countries—such as Austria, Japan, the Netherlands and West Germany in the case of the basic oxygen process, and the United Kingdom in the case of nuclear power.[32] Thus, although the United States seemed to be relatively quick, on the average, to accept most of these innovations, it was not always a leader in this regard.

COSTS OF AMMONIA PRODUCTION WITH OLDER TYPES OF PLANTS

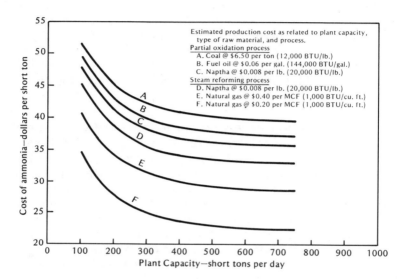

Estimated production cost as related to plant capacity, type of raw material, and process.

Partial oxidation process
A. Coal @ $6.50 per ton (12,000 BTU/lb.)
B. Fuel oil @ $0.06 per gal. (144,000 BTU/gal.)
C. Naptha @ $0.008 per lb. (20,000 BTU/lb.)

Steam reforming process
D. Naptha @ $0.008 per lb. (20,000 BTU/lb.)
E. Natural gas @ $0.40 per MCF (1,000 BTU/cu. ft.)
F. Natural gas @ $0.20 per MCF (1,000 BTU/cu. ft.)

Source: D. Bixby, D. Rucker and S. Tisdale, *Phosphatic Fertilizers: Properties and Processes*, Technical Bulletin No. 8 (Washington, D.C.: The Sulphur Institute, February 1964). Reprinted by permission of the Sulphur Institute.

114

APPENDIX TABLE 5-1

DETAILED ECONOMIC ANALYSIS OF INVESTMENT IN NUMERICALLY CONTROLLED MACHINE TOOLS, TWELVE TOOL AND DIE SHOPS

	Firm 1			Firm 2		Firm 3
	Machine 1	Machine 2	Machine 3	Machine 1	Machine 2	Machine 1
First cost	$ 70,000	$ 12,000	$ 14,000	$ 20,000	$ 135,000	$ 39,000
Number of conventional machines displaced	3	1	1	3	1	3
Savings in jigs and fixtures per year	$ 5,000	$ 2,000	$ 3,000	$ 5,000	$ 4,000	--
Savings in direct labor hours per year	1,250 hrs	1,000 hrs	1,200 hrs	4,000 hrs	1,500 hrs	2,000 hrs
Savings in inspection per year	--	--	--	--	$ 300	$ 8,000
Savings in scrap per year	$ 2,000	$ 1,000	$ 500	$ 2,000	--	$ 600
Savings in inventory	$ 20,000	$ 20,000	$ 20,000	--	--	--
Savings in floor space	20 sq.ft.	--	--	40 sq.ft.	--	--
Savings in cost of materials handling	$ 1,000	--	--	--	$ 800	$ 15,000
Extra cost of maintenance per year	$ 1,000	--	$ 1,000	$ 2,000	$ 30,000	$ 500
Training cost	$ 2,000	$ 500	$ 500	$ 1,200	$ 1,200	$ 1,300
Programming cost per year	$ 1,500	$ 500	$ 500	$ 8,000	$ 4,000	$ 3,750
Estimated life (in years)	20	20	20	8	12	10

APPENDIX TABLE 5-1 (continued)

	Firm 4 Machine 1	Firm 5[a] Machine 1	Firm 6 Machine 1	Firm 7 Machine 1	Firm 8 Machine 1	Firm 9 Machine 1
First cost	$ 50,000	$ 48,000	$ 45,000	$ 55,000	$ 55,000	$ 35,000
Number of conventional machines displaced	3	1.25	4	2.5	1.5	4
Savings in jigs and fixtures per year	$ 10,000	--	$ 50,000	--	--	$ 20,000
Savings in direct labor hours per year	4,000 hrs	600 hrs	3,000 hrs	3,000 hrs	1,250 hrs	7,500 hrs
Savings in inspection per year	$ 4,000	--	$ 4,000	$ 300	--	$ 3,000
Savings in scrap per year	--	--	$ 2,000	--	$ 750	$ 5,000
Savings in inventory	$ 20,000	--	--	--	--	--
Savings in floor space	136 sq.ft.	--	20 sq.ft.	200 sq.ft.	8 sq.ft.	100 sq.ft.
Savings in cost of materials handling	$ 1,200	--	$ 6,000	--	--	$ 1,000
Extra cost of maintenance per year	$ 2,000	$ 500	--	$ 100	$ 200	--
Training cost	$ 1,000	$ 400	$ 4,000	$ 400	$ 1,000	$ 5,000
Programming cost per year	$ 1,500	nil	$ 11,000	$ 500	$ 500	$ 9,000
Estimated life (years)	10	10	10	15	6	10

APPENDIX TABLE 5-1 (continued)

	Firm 10		Firm 11		Firm 12	
	Machine 1	Machine 2	Machine 1	Machine 2	Machine 1	Machine 2
First cost	$125,000	$135,000	$ 15,000	b	$ 12,000	$ 35,000
Number of conventional machines displaced	3	3	3	6	2	3
Savings in jigs and fixtures per year	$ 35,000	$ 35,000	$ 11,000	--	$ 7,000	$ 20,000
Savings in direct labor hours per year	1,500 hrs	1,500 hrs	5,000 hrs	25,000 hrs	2,500 hrs	5,000 hrs
Savings in inspection per yr.	--	--	$ 500	$ 2,000	$ 3,000	$ 7,500
Savings in scrap per year	$ 15,000	$ 15,000	$ 2,000	$ 2,000	--	--
Savings in inventory	$ 35,000	$ 35,000	--	--	--	--
Savings in floor space	1,000 sq.ft.	1,000 sq.ft.	300 sq.ft.	3,000 sq.ft.	80 sq.ft.	150 sq.ft.
Savings in cost of materials handling	--	--	--	$ 8,000	$ 2,000	$ 4,000
Extra cost of maintenance per year	$ 12,000	$ 12,000	$ 200	$ 3,000	--	--
Training cost	$ 6,000	$ 4,000	$ 200	$ 10,000	$ 2,000	$ 3,000
Programming cost per year	$ 4,000	$ 4,000	$ 1,000	$ 8,000	$ 10,000	$ 35,000
Estimated life (years)	15	15	10	10	9	14

Source: Interviews. Blank spaces denote negligible estimated savings or costs.

[a]Firm 5 had not yet begun using its N.C. equipment. These are merely the firm's estimates of what it will save.

[b]This is a very large and expensive piece of N.C. equipment, the exact cost of which is not reported because the firm preferred that it be omitted.

117

TABULATION OF DATA ON THE DIFFUSION OF EIGHT INDUSTRIAL INNOVATIONS SHOWN
GRAPHICALLY IN CHARTS 5-1 THROUGH 5-5 AND CHARTS 5-7 THROUGH 5-10

Year	Value of shipments; numerically controlled machine tools as percent of all metal cutting machine tools	Percent of steel output produced by basic oxygen process	Catalytic cracking capacity as percent of total U.S. petroleum cracking capacity (data discontinued after 1957)	Capacity of large-scale ammonia plants (600 tons/day or more) as percent of U.S. total ammonia capacity	Percent of acrylonitrile output produced from propylene	Percent of U.S. vinyl chloride capacity that uses oxychlorination process	Value of output; discrete semiconductors as percent of discrete semiconductors and receiving tubes	Nuclear capacity as percent of all installed electrical generating capacity	Increase in capacity; nuclear capacity as percent of all new capacity installed
	(1)	(2)	(3)	(4)	(5)	(6)	(7)	(8)	(9)
1937	-	-	0.1	-	-	-	-	-	-
1938	-	-	0.6	-	-	-	-	-	-
1939	-	-	1.1	-	-	-	-	-	-
1940	-	-	5.6	-	-	-	-	-	-
1941	-	-	6.6	-	-	-	-	-	-
1942	-	-	7.0	-	-	-	-	-	-
1943	-	-	9.9	-	-	-	-	-	-
1944	-	-	21.4	-	-	-	-	-	-
1945	-	-	28.5	-	-	-	-	-	-
1946	-	-	30.0	-	-	-	-	-	-
1947	-	-	32.2	-	-	-	-	-	-
1948	-	-	34.0	-	-	-	-	-	-
1949	-	-	37.4	-	-	-	-	-	-
1950	-	-	41.7	-	-	-	-	-	-
1951	-	-	43.8	-	-	-	-	-	-
1952	-	-	46.7	-	-	-	6.4	-	-
1953	-	-	61.2	-	-	-	7.4	-	-
1954	-	-	67.5	-	-	-	8.0	-	-
1955	-	-	74.7	-	-	-	9.5	-	-
1956	-	-	79.3	-	-	-	18.8	-	-
1957	-	-	81.9	-	-	-	27.4	-	-
1958	-	1.6	-	-	-	-	-	-	-
1959	3.7	2.0	-	-	-	-	51.4	0.1	-
1960	6.4	3.4	-	-	9.1	-	60.9	0.2	-
1961	9.1	4.0	-	-	11.2	-	63.3	0.2	-
1962	10.2	5.6	-	-	15.3	-	64.2	0.4	-
1963	13.0	7.8	-	-	22.0	-	68.2	0.4	-
1964	12.1	12.2	-	-	32.6	-	71.5	0.5	-
1965	15.2	17.4	-	2.5	46.0	32.0	76.1	0.5	-
1966	20.0	25.3	-	6.2	59.5	40.0	79.0	0.7	-
1967	21.0	32.6	-	20.1	86.0	-	81.4	1.0	-
1968	27.1	37.1	-	41.7	88.9	56.0	82.3	0.9	-
1969	23.6	42.6	-	58.3	89.7	70.0	-	1.3	5.0
1970	19.0	48.2	-	58.8	94.7	-	-	2.1	9.0
1971	21.4	53.1	-	63.1	100.0	81.0	-	2.6	8.0
1972	21.7	56.0	-	-	-	83.0	-	3.6	21.0
1973	21.0	55.2	-	-	-	-	-	4.4	15.0
1974	25.0	56.0	-	79.2	-	-	-	6.7	28.0

Sources: (1) E. Schwartz and T. Prenting, "Automation in the Fabricating Industries" in Report of the National Commission on Technology, Automation, and Economic Progress, Vol. I, 1966, p. 316; and Current Industrial Reports, U.S. Department of Commerce, 1966-74. (2) American Iron and Steel Institute. (3) Oil and Gas Journal, various issues. (4) Stanford Research Institute. (5) Stanford Research Institute. (6) Oil Paint, and Drug Reporter, October 18, 1965, April 29, 1968, March 17, 1969, October 11, 1971; R. Stobaugh, Petrochemical Manufacturing and Marketing Guide, Gulf, 1968; and D. Keane, R. Stobaugh and P. Townsend, "Vinyl Chloride," Hydrocarbon Processing, February 1973. (7) Business and Defense Services Administration; and J. Tilton, International Diffusion of Technology: The Case of Semiconductors (Washington, D.C.: Brookings, 1971). (8) Statistical Abstract of the United States and Federal Power Commission. (9) Edison Electric Institute and Federal Power Commission.

Notes

1 For a summary of the literature, see Edwin Mansfield, "Determinants of the Speed of Application of New Technology," ed. C.R. Williams, *Science and Technology in Economy Growth* (New York: Macmillan Co., 1973).

2 For more technical studies, and ones that emphasize analysis rather than description, see Edwin Mansfield, *Industrial Research and Technological Innovation* (New York: W.W. Norton and Co., 1968); "Technical Change and the Rate of Imitation," *Econometrica* (October 1961); "The Speed of Response of Firms to New Techniques," *Quarterly Journal of Economics* (May 1963); "Intrafirm Rates of Diffusion of an Innovation," *Review of Economics and Statistics* (November 1963); and Edwin Mansfield, John Rapoport, J. Schnee, Samuel Wagner and M. Hamburger, *Research and Innovation in the Modern Corporation* (New York: W.W. Norton and Co., 1971).

3 Letter from Everard Munsey, National Planning Association, April 21, 1975.

4 These results were obtained by Anthony Romeo in the course of his doctoral work at the University of Pennsylvania.

5 Edwin Mansfield, *Numerical Control: Diffusion and Impact in the Tool and Die Industry* (Small Business Administration, 1968). Some of the earlier paragraphs of this section are taken from this source.

6 A. Gebhardt and O. Hatzold, "Numerically Controlled Machine Tools," in L. Nabseth and G. Ray, *The Diffusion of New Industrial Processes* (New York and Cambridge: Cambridge University Press, 1974).

7 J. Metyer and G. Herregat, "The Basic Oxygen Steel Process," in *The Diffusion of New Industrial Processes*.

8 G. Maddala and P. Knight, "International Diffusion of Technical Change: A Case Study of the Oxygen Steel-Making Process," *Economic Journal* (September 1967).

9 J. Dirlam and W. Adams, "Big Steel, Invention, and Innovation," *Quarterly Journal of Economics* (May 1966).

10 D. Dilley and D. McBride, "Oxygen Steelmaking—Fact vs. Folklore," *Iron and Steel Engineer* (October 1967). See also A. McAdams, "Big Steel: Invention and Innovation Reconsidered," *Quarterly Journal of Economics* (August 1967).

11 C. Tsao and R. Day, "A Process Analysis Model of the U.S. Steel Industry," *Management Science* (June 1971).

12 B. Gold, W. Peirce and G. Rosegger, "Diffusion of Major Technological Innovations in U.S. Iron and Steel Manufacturing," *Journal of Industrial Economics* (July 1970).

13 John Enos, *Petroleum Progress and Profits* (Cambridge, Mass: M.I.T. Press, 1962); and Enos, "Invention and Innovation in the Petroleum Refining Industry," in *The Rate and Direction of Inventive Activity* (New York: National Bureau of Economic Research, 1962).

14 *Business Week*, November 13, 1965.

15 *Chemical Economics Handbook* (Stanford Research Institute, 1969).

16 Ibid., 703.4310D and 703.4302.

17 This result came about as part of Peter Simon's doctoral work at the University of Pennsylvania. This section, as well as the sections on ammonia plants and oxychlorination, are based partly on his work.

18 *Chemical Economics Handbook*, 607.5032F.

19 OECD, *Gaps in Technology: Plastics* (Paris, 1969).

20 D. Keane, R. Stobaugh and P. Townsend, "Vinyl Chloride," *Hydrocarbon Processing* (February 1973).

21 For a variety of reasons, the figures in the late 1960s may be rough, but they seem to be sufficiently accurate for present purposes.

22 See OECD, *Gaps in Technology: Electronic Components* (Paris, 1968); and R. Nelson, "The Link Between Science and Invention: The Case of the Transistor," in *The Rate and Direction of Inventive Activity.*

23 John Tilton, *International Diffusion of Technology: The Case of Semiconductors* (Washington, D.C.: Brookings, 1971). I am indebted to Tilton for providing me with some of his basic data.

24 Some of the material in this section has benefited from an unpublished paper by K. Mayland, a graduate student at the University of Pennsylvania.

25 Joint Committee on Atomic Energy, *Nuclear Power and Related Energy Problems*, 1968-70 (U.S. Congress, 1971). Of course, there have been many later publications on this score. For example, see *Business Week*, November 17, 1975.

26 OECD, *Gaps in Technology: Analytical Report* (Paris, 1970).

27 Enos, *Petroleum Progress and Profits*, p. 154.

28 Meyer and Herregat, "The Basic Oxygen Steel Process."

29 Dilley and McBride, "Oxygen Steelmaking."

30 Gold, Peirce and Rosegger, "Diffusion of Major Technological Innovations."

31 This is part of Simon's doctoral work at the University of Pennsylvania.

32 As a crude measure of the rate of acceptance, we used the percent of steel output from oxygen converters in 1969. In the case of nuclear power, we used the percent of all the power capacity installed in 1964-67 that was nuclear. Note that this measure for nuclear power pertains only to 1964-67, the period used by OECD in the source cited in note 26.

6 Estimates of the Direct and Indirect Effects of Industrial R&D on Economic Growth

Nestor E. Terleckyj

Introduction

This chapter attempts to construct quantitative estimates of the effects of R&D on economic growth based on the available results of economic research in this field. While only tentative and rather speculative estimates of these effects can be made at present, sufficient evidence exists about the nature and magnitude of the effects of R&D on growth to warrant an attempt to begin to organize the existing research results into quantitative indicators, and, as more knowledge becomes available, to improve and refine them.

The estimates are presented here in the form of an annual time series of the value, in constant dollars, of growth in the national output (GNP) attributed to the conduct of industrial R&D. A series of assumptions is involved in constructing the estimates. These assumptions are necessary to establish a link between the existing estimates of the effects of R&D on growth, usually given as rates of return to R&D investment realized over a particular time period in a given set of industries or firms, and the global estimates of the contribution of industrial R&D activities to the growth of the whole economy in a series of particular years. These assumptions involve, among others, the choice of particular estimates of the rate of return to R&D, the scope of their applicability to other industries and other periods, and the treatment of government financed R&D. They are discussed in detail in the last section of this chapter. These assumptions can be modified. Indeed, plausible assumptions could have been made over a considerable range of variation at many steps, both in interpreting the available research results and in applying them to the development of annual growth indicators.

The resulting estimates are definitely experimental. At present, precise observations are not possible for measuring, on an ongoing basis, the contribution of research and development activities to economic growth. However, the results of several different research studies conducted in this field are sufficiently consistent to provide strong evidence, which cannot be dismissed, that there are substantial economic returns to industrial R&D activities, and further that these returns are realized not only by the firms (and industries) in which the R&D is conducted, but also, and possibly even in a greater measure, by the purchasers of the products of those firms (and industries). Evidence supporting the existence of such returns is available only for privately financed R&D. Statistical analysis does not support the hypothesis that there are comparable returns to government financed R&D. Consequently, all the estimates presented here are based only on the possible effects of privately financed R&D on economic growth.

In the next section of this chapter, the results of a study by the author are summarized and compared with the results of other studies which have also addressed the question of the productivity returns to R&D in the industries conducting R&D and in the industries using R&D-intensive products. Because productivity growth is a component of economic growth (other components being growth in the amounts of labor and of capital), the contribution of R&D to economic growth consists of its contribution to productivity growth.

Available Research Results

A number of research studies have established the existence of statistical links between research intensity (volume of R&D activity relative to volume of output) and productivity growth at the level of groups of companies or industries.[1] These studies found that, to a significant extent, variations in productivity growth could be explained statistically by the differences in the rates of R&D investment as well as by certain other variables. Plausible estimates of the magnitudes of the effects of R&D were developed. Many of the studies, including earlier research by the author,[2] are based on an analytical model in which research and development is treated as a distinct form of capital, and is introduced in the statistical analysis as a third factor of production along with labor and physical capital. In these studies, the productivity rate of return on research capital is estimated statistically as a component of productivity growth. Other variables known to affect productivity growth are also included in order to obtain estimates of the effects of R&D on productivity unaffected by their influence. The underlying theoretical model has been discussed by Griliches and in the study already cited by the author and will not be discussed again here.[3]

To summarize briefly the author's study, the relationship between change in total factor productivity and research and development was investigated by means of a then new and rather substantial body of data on total factor productivity compiled by John W. Kendrick for 33 manufacturing and nonmanufacturing industries covering the period 1948-66.[4] At the time, these were the only industries with available estimates of total factor productivity.

Most of the past studies attempted to relate R&D conducted in an industry to productivity growth in the same industry. However, two earlier studies, one by Brown and Conrad and another by Raines, attempted to estimate the effects of R&D on the productivity of industries purchasing products from industries conducting R&D.[5] In these two studies, the R&D expenditures were redistributed among industries by means of an input-output matrix.

Although the existence of external effects of R&D was suspected and explored in the earlier studies, no explicit analysis was undertaken to systematically and simultaneously examine the possible effects on productivity of (1) R&D conducted in the industries versus R&D conducted by the industries supplying their capital and intermediate goods, and (2) privately financed R&D versus government financed R&D. The author undertook to examine systematically the possibilities of differential R&D effects by developing R&D intensity ratios for the four categories of R&D and by testing them, along with a series of control variables, on the newly developed productivity data.

Specifically, the author's study was concerned with estimating the rates of return to R&D measured as components of growth in industrial productivity. These returns were estimated as the coefficients b_j in the following regression equation:

$$p = a_o + \sum_{i=1}^{n} a_i X_i + \sum_{j=1}^{4} b_j I_j + u$$

where p is the annual rate of growth of total factor productivity as measured by Kendrick for the period 1948-66, a_o is the constant of the regression, X_i the variables other than the R&D ratios significantly affecting productivity growth and introduced to hold constant their effects, a_i the coefficients measuring their effects, I_j the four R&D intensity ratios of R&D expenditure to value added for 1958, and u the remaining unexplained variation. The coefficients b_j are the estimates of the marginal products of the respective types of R&D capital, and they also represent the productivity rates of return on the different types of R&D expenditures. In the estimating equation, the intensity ratios for the different types of R&D capital times the marginal products of these types of capital given bj, the coefficients bj are additive components of the productivity growth rate. These coefficients are the unknowns to be estimated from the equation and are the main objects of this research.

Because the costs of labor and capital used in R&D are already included in the input index used to estimate productivity, the regression coefficient b_j measures the "excess" or additional rates of return to R&D, i.e., the net of its cost. Thus, the statistical estimates of the productivity rates of return approximate the concept of "internal rates of return." An internal rate of return is that interest rate which will make equal a time stream of cost and a time stream of income. The accuracy of the statistical approximation depends on the extent to which the cost and the effects of same R&D projects are included in the data for the period used.

Given the analytical model underlying this research and a series of assumptions which were made regarding the applicability of the model (and are discussed in greater length in the full study cited), a coefficient of regression relating an R&D intensity ratio to the rate of productivity growth (which represents the average annual increase in the output-input ratio for the period) approximates the productivity rate of return per unit of R&D investment, with both variables being normalized to the size of the industry as measured by inputs. The coefficient, then, links the rate of growth of output relative to input to the rate of growth of R&D capital also relative to input. (For productivity, output equals input in the base period.) The rates of producitivity growth estimated by Kendrick and the four R&D intensity ratios (government versus privately financed and direct R&D versus R&D attributed through purchases) are shown in Table 6-1.[6] The estimating procedures underlying the data in Table 6-1 are described in the sources cited.

Research and development, of course, is not the only factor which may affect productivity growth. Previous research has established statistical relationships between productivity growth and a number of other factors. Initially, three such variables have been included in the regression equations to hold constant their effects: (1) proportion of total industry sales to nongovernment customers, introduced by the author as an explanatory variable; (2) unionization rate of industry workers, which Kendrick found to be correlated with productivity growth; and (3) cyclical instability of industry output, found to have a significant correlation with productivity growth in an earlier study by the author.[7] These variables have been included in all the statistical analyses of the relationship between R&D and productivity growth.

In addition to these variables, productivity growth could be affected by increases in "human capital" (productive skills), as a number of earlier studies indicate. The productive capability of workers is not measured as part of the labor input in the productivity measurement system, which uses simply the number of man-hours worked. Increases in human capital have been measured by economists in terms of amount of education (years of schooling or number of academic degrees attained) or years of experience. They can also be measured by increases in wages, on the basis of the theory of correspondence between productivity and wages brought about by the mobility of workers.

If the use of larger amounts of human capital is correlated with the use of more R&D inputs, direct or purchased, then omitting human capital from the estimating equation results in an estimate of the rate of return to R&D that may be inflated insofar as it reflects increased output resulting from increased use of human capital. (It is also possible that the two are so highly correlated

TABLE 6-1

RATES OF GROWTH IN TOTAL FACTOR PRODUCTIVITY 1948-66, AND THE 1958
R&D VALUE ADDED RATIOS FOR THE R&D FOR PRIVATELY FINANCED R&D AND FOR
GOVERNMENT FINANCED R&D CONDUCTED IN THE INDUSTRY AND FOR
PRIVATELY FINANCED AND GOVERNMENT FINANCED R&D EMBODIED IN PURCHASED GOODS,
33 INDUSTRIES IN THE PRIVATE DOMESTIC ECONOMY
(R&D amounts as percent of value added)

Industry (Arranged in order of descending productivity growth)	Productivity growth rate, annual average 1948-66	R&D Intensity Ratios, 1958			
		R&D conducted in industry		R&D embodied in purchased goods	
		Privately financed R&D	Government financed R&D	Privately financed R&D	Government financed R&D
*Air transportation	8.0%	0%	0%	1.6%	1.5%
*Coal mining	5.2	0	0	.3	.1
*Railroads	5.2	0	0	.2	.1
Chemicals	4.9	8.6	6.8	1.8	.8
*Electric and gas utilities	4.9	.1	.1	.3	.3
Textiles	4.0	.4	.4	2.1	.1
Rubber products	3.9	1.5	1.1	2.3	.3
*Communication utilities	3.8	.4	.3	.6	1.1
Electrical machinery	3.7	17.5	5.5	1.9	3.3
Lumber products	3.5	.2	.2	.3	.1
*Farming	3.3	.5	.5	.6	.1
*Oil and gas extraction	3.2	.2	.2	.1	.1
Transportation equipment & ordnance	3.2	25.5	6.9	3.8	3.8
Foods	3.0	.5	.5	.6	.1
Petroleum refining	3.0	4.5	4.3	.9	.3
Furniture	2.9	.2	.2	.4	.1
Instruments	2.9	7.8	4.2	2.1	2.2
Printing and publishing	2.7	0	0	.2	.2
Machinery, excluding electric	2.6	6.2	3.7	1.1	.9
*Nonmetal mining	2.6	0	0	.4	.1
Paper	2.5	.9	.9	.5	.1
*Wholesale trade	2.5	0	0	.1	.1
*Metal mining	2.4	0	0	.4	.2
*Retail trade	2.4	0	0	.1	.1
Stone, clay and glass products	2.4	.9	.9	.5	.1
Beverages	2.2	.3	0	.6	.1
Apparel	1.9	.1	.1	.3	0
Fabricated metal products	1.9	1.2	.7	.7	.3
Leather products	1.7	.2	.2	.2	.1
Primary metal products	1.6	1.0	.9	.6	.2
*Contract construction	1.5	0	0	.6	.3
Tobacco products	1.1	0	0	.3	0
*Water transportation	0.5	0	0	.4	0

*Nonmanufacturing industries.

Sources: Productivity Growth Rate data reproduced by permission from the author: John W.
Kendrick, Postwar Productivity Trends in the United States, 1948-1969 (New York: National
Bureau of Economic Research, 1973), Table 5-1, pp. 78-79; R&D intensity ratios from Nestor
E. Terleckyj, Effects of R&D on the Productivity Growth of Industries: An Exploratory Study
(Washington, D.C.: National Planning Association, 1974), pp. 13-15. (Note revision of data for
beverages industry R&D conducted in industry ratios.)

that they appear as joint inputs, and thus separate attribution to human capital and to R&D capital cannot be made).

In addition to human capital, output may also increase as a result of improvements of physical capital not related to R&D. Improvements of physical capital related to R&D conducted in capital goods industries are already reflected in purchased R&D. But, historically, the productivity of capital was growing even before the age of organized research. Many improvements may still result independently of the conduct of R&D in the capital goods industries. It is important to test this "pure vintage" hypothesis of the non-R&D-capital modernization effects. However, productivity effects of the rejuvenation of capital apart from R&D may be correlated with the increased use of R&D capital. Both are likely to be greatest when the rate of investment is highest. Separating the two effects may, therefore, be quite difficult.

The results of the author's 1974 study were obtained without the use of either human capital or a vintage modernization variable. In the subsequent 1975 study (see note 2), these results were tested by the introduction of a human capital variable. But it has not been practical as yet to test the vintage modernization hypothesis because of lack of sufficiently detailed industry data.

Introduction of the human capital variable did not change the previous estimates of returns to R&D. The human capital variable was measured by the growth in real wage scaled for the size of employment and expressed as the human capital investment intensity ratio. (Some problems attach to the use of growth of the real wage as an explanatory variable because statistical biases may result from possible causal effects of productivity growth on wages in the same industries. However, the study period is probably sufficiently long for the tendency toward a uniformity of wages among industries for comparable categories of workers to overcome the shorter-term effects of productivity changes on wages in the particular industries.)

Data used in the study for variables other than R&D, i.e., sales to nongovernment customers, unionization rate, indicator of cyclical instability and the human capital investment intensity ratio, are shown in Table 6-2.

TABLE 6-2

VARIABLES OTHER THAN R&D TESTED FOR POSSIBLE EFFECTS ON PRODUCTIVITY GROWTH, 33 INDUSTRIES IN THE PRIVATE DOMESTIC ECONOMY

Industry (Arranged in order of descending productivity growth)	Sales Other than to Government as Percent of Total Sales 1958 PVTS	Union Members as Percent of All Workers in Producing Establishments 1953 UN	Index of Cyclical Instability of Industry Outputs 1948-66 CYC	Human Capital Investment Intensity Ratio. Average Annual Increase in Real Wages Paid as Percent of Value-added, 1958
*Air transportation	95%	51%	0%	2.4%
*Coal mining	98	84	16.1	1.6
*Railroads	95	95	10.4	2.6
Chemicals	95	39	5.7	1.9
*Electric and gas utilities	96	41	0	1.2
Textiles	100	30	7.4	1.5
Rubber products	97	54	9.5	1.6
*Communication utilities	97	52	0	1.6
Electrical machinery	90	56	11.0	2.0
Lumber products	100	21	8.7	2.1
*Farming	98	1	3.2	1.0
*Oil and gas extraction	100	14	5.4	0.5
Transportation equipment and ordnance	77	65	11.0	2.6
Foods	100	45	0	1.9
Petroleum refining	94	67	2.5	2.0
Furniture	95	29	8.7	1.9
Instruments	85	50	9.2	2.3
Printing and publishing	98	38	3.2	1.3
Machinery, excluding electric	95	45	13.1	2.1
*Nonmetal mining	99	32	4.6	1.9
Paper	99	45	6.7	1.9
*Wholesale trade	99	4	4.1	1.6
*Metal mining	92	70	10.6	1.4
*Retail trade	99	14	3.6	2.0
Stone, clay and glass products	100	45	7.4	2.0
Beverages	100	44	3.2	1.0
Apparel	99	53	4.1	1.3
Fabricated metal products	99	45	8.4	2.0
Leather products	99	39	5.0	1.6
Primary metal products	98	55	15.2	2.3
*Contract construction	71	72	4.1	3.0
Tobacco products	100	58	2.0	.6
*Water transportation	95	76	7.0	2.9

*Nonmanufacturing industry.

Sources: Data on industry sales to government is from: U.S. Department of Commerce, Office of Business Economics, "The Transactions Table of the 1958 Input-Output Study and Revised Direct and Total Requirements Data," Survey of Current Business, Vol. 45, No. 9, September 1965, pp. 34-39; Percent unionization is from H.G. Lewis, Unionization and Wages in the United States (Chicago: University of Chicago Press, 1963), pp. 289-290.
Cyclical instability index of industry output is based on annual output data from John W. Kendrick, Postwar Productivity Trends in the United States, 1948-1969 (New York: National Bureau of Economic Research, 1973) calculated in a manner described in Nestor E. Terleckyj, "Source of Productivity Advance. A Pilot Study of Manufacturing Industries, 1899-1953," Ph.D. Dissertation, Columbia University, 1960, pp. 111-113. See note 6, p. 16, in Terleckyj, Effects of R&D.
Human capital investment intensity ratios, their theoretical rationale and derivation of data are discussed in Terleckyj, "Direct and Indirect Effects of Industrial Research and Development on the Productivity of Industries," paper given at the November 1975 Conference on Research in Income and Wealth, to appear in a forthcoming volume New Developments in Productivity Measurement, published by the National Bureau of Economic Research in their series on Research in Income and Wealth.

The statistical results obtained by the author are summarized in Table 6-3. The table shows estimates of the statistical equation discussed at the beginning of this section, obtained with different sets of variables and for different groupings of industries.

The strongest results are obtained in equation 3. In that equation, a strong, significant coefficient is obtained for privately financed R&D conducted in industry, suggesting a 28 percent productivity return to privately financed R&D. In the same equation, the productivity return to privately financed R&D embodied in purchases from other industries is estimated at 78 percent. In that equation, after correcting for the number of degrees of freedom, 73 percent of interindustry variation in productivity growth among the 20 manufacturing industries is explained. Significant coefficients of the theoretically expected sign are obtained for the three non-R&D variables. The coefficients for government financed R&D are not statistically significant, and the coefficient for government financed R&D performed in industry is actually negative. The coefficient for the human capital investment intensity ratio (constructed by the same method as the R&D investment intensity ratios) is not statistically significant, although it suggests a 38 percent rate of productivity return to human capital.

Such strong results are obtained only, for the manufacturing industries. As can be seen in Table 6-3, the results are much weaker for the 13 nonmanufacturing industries and for all the industries taken together.

In the nonmanufacturing industries, government financed direct R&D is negligible (see Table 6-1), and the variable is omitted from the equation. There is some indication of possibly large but not statistically significant returns for indirect R&D obtained for these industries.

The results for all 33 industries taken together are also erratic. A statistically significant and negative coefficient is obtained for the government financed R&D conducted in industry, while the coefficients for the two indirect R&D ratios are statistically significant and positive. The dummy variable for nonmanufacturing is the strongest variable, suggesting that the most important explanatory factor for the differences in productivity growth

TABLE 6-3

REGRESSION COEFFICIENTS OBTAINED IN THE ANALYSIS OF THE ANNUAL RATES
OF CHANGE IN TOTAL FACTOR PRODUCTIVITY FOR THE PERIOD 1948-66,
33 MANUFACTURING AND NONMANUFACTURING INDUSTRIES
(t-ratios in parentheses)

Equation Number	Constant of Regression	R&D Conducted in Industry — Privately Financed, 1958	R&D Conducted in Industry — Government Financed, 1958	R&D Embodied in Purchases from Other Industries — Privately Financed, 1958	R&D Embodied in Purchases from Other Industries — Government Financed, 1958	Percent of Sales not to Government, 1958	Union Members as Percent of Workers in Producing Establishments, 1953	Annual Rate of Cyclical Change in Output, 1948-66	Human Capital Investment Intensity Ratio, 1958	Dummy Variable for Nonmanufacturing	R^2 Corrected
20 MANUFACTURING INDUSTRIES											
(1)	-3.60 (.67)	.28 (3.06)	-.05 (.55)	.80 (3.68)	.10 (.21)	.08 (1.46)	-.04 (3.75)	-.04 (1.25)			.69
(2)	-6.17 (1.02)	.25 (2.50)	-.05 (.59)	.85 (3.78)	.17 (.37)	.10 (1.70)	-.04 (3.41)	-.07 (1.56)	.38 (.93)		.69
(3)	-4.74 (1.21)	.28 (3.49)		.77 (3.85)		.09 (2.41)	-.05 (4.12)	-.04 (1.38)			.73
13 NONMANUFACTURING INDUSTRIES											
(4)	-7.37 (.84)	-.18 (.05)		1.10 (.43)	2.66 (1.02)	.09 (1.05)	-.00 (.09)	.12 (1.58)			.16
(5)	-4.47 (.46)	-2.27 (.49)		2.04 (.71)	1.68 (.57)	.08 (.87)	.02 (.51)	.03 (.12)	-1.05 (.80)		.11
33 MANUFACTURING AND NONMANUFACTURING INDUSTRIES											
(6)	-4.80 (.82)	-.10 (.52)	-.37 (2.23)	.72 (1.47)	1.73 (2.43)	.07 (1.29)	.01 (.61)	-.01 (.19)	-.03 (.06)		.14
(7)	-9.46 (1.72)	.08 (.42)	-.32 (2.13)	1.04 (2.24)	1.31 (2.00)	.11 (2.14)	.01 (.82)	.00 (.08)	-.04 (.83)	1.43 (2.67)	.31

within these industries is whether they are classified as manufacturing or nonmanufacturing. For these reasons, the results cannot be accepted as reliable estimates. However, results for manufacturing industries are statistically significant and correspond to the results obtained by other investigators.

The estimates obtained in equation 3 for the manufacturing industries represent the best evidence obtained by the author on the magnitude of the economic growth effects which may be traced to industrial research. The estimated returns are rounded to 30 percent for the direct privately financed returns and 80 percent for the indirect returns, i.e., returns to R&D embodied in purchases. Zero returns are accepted for the government financed R&D, both direct or indirect, because the equations for the manufacturing industries that appear to be both internally strongest and most consistent with the theoretical *a priori* reasoning, as well as with other evidence, do not suggest such returns. This does not necessarily mean that the possibility of economic growth effects which could be traced directly or indirectly to the government financed R&D is rejected out of hand. Rather, it means that insofar as statistical evidence is concerned, the possibility that such returns do not exist cannot be rejected. The hints of their existence and their magnitude are very uncertain, because those hints occur in equations which are suspect for other reasons.

In interpreting the results obtained by the author, the results of two sets of studies by two other investigators are particularly important. One is an analysis by Griliches based on econometric examination of return to productivity growth in a large number of companies in five different industries together with his earlier study of the effects of R&D in 85 manufacturing industries.[8] The other is a study by Mansfield of the rates of return to innovation expenditures. This study deals with 17 innovations adapted in a number of different industries in which both direct returns to the innovating firm and social returns, including the values realized by other firms and by consumers, are estimated.[9] The results obtained by Griliches and Mansfield suggest magnitudes of the direct returns similar to those obtained by the author. But Mansfield's estimates of the indirect returns are lower than the author's, though still quite high. The two earlier econometric studies of indirect returns by Brown and Conrad and by Raines, mentioned before, were formulated in terms which do not permit comparisons with the rates of return estimated elsewhere. It should be noted, however, that in both cases statistically significant relationships between productivity growth and indirect R&D were identified.

In his 1975 study, Griliches reported the results of research conducted over a series of years in which he analyzed a large volume of data given him by the Census Bureau in processed form to preserve confidentiality. The study undertook to measure, among other things, the profit rate of return to R&D

conducted in industry for a sample of 883 companies representing very high proportions of all industrial R&D conducted. The data were also broken down separately into five industries. In this study, Griliches explored a number of formulations of R&D variables as well as the relationship between R&D and various company performance variables including profits and productivity. For the whole observation period 1957-65 and for all industries combined, he found a highly significant effect of the R&D variables. He obtained an estimate of implied elasticity of output with respect to accumulated R&D of about .07. The results were consistent for different analytical formulations (growth equations vs. level equations). He estimated a 17 percent rate of return to total R&D, i.e., company and government financed, in the combined equation for companies in all industries. Of the six industries, he obtained a 93 percent rate of return in one industry (chemicals); in three industries (metals and machinery, motor vehicles and "other"), the rates were 23 to 25 percent; in two industries (electrical equipment, and aircraft and missiles), the rates of return were very low, 2 and 5 percent, respectively. These industries have much higher proportions of government financed R&D than the other four industries. In the other four industries, most of the R&D was privately financed, and the estimates obtained may be interpreted as approximations to returns to private expenditure for R&D.

In the 1973 study, Griliches estimated the productivity rate of return to R&D using data for 85 manufacturing industries (defined at a more detailed level than the 20 industries in the author's study) for the period 1958-63. He obtained estimates of rates of return of 32 to 40 percent to privately financed R&D. The study by the author for 20 manufacturing industries gave an estimate of 37 percent productivity return to privately financed R&D when only direct R&D inputs were considered. Thus, the results of the two studies are consistent.

The study by Manfield and his associates attempted to estimate private and social rates of return to R&D. It involved a careful and detailed examination of R&D, sales, production, marketing and financial records of cooperating companies performing innovations, data for their customer industries, consumption data for households, and information on competing industries, firms and products. The rates of return were estimated for the expenditures for all innovation activities, which included R&D and associated investment and marketing expenditures. For the 17 innovations studied, Mansfield and his associates found a median social rate of return of 55 percent and a median private rate of return of 25 percent. Though Mansfield's concepts are not quite comparable with the author's, he too considered only private expenditures for R&D. But he included other catagories of innovation expenditure and other external cost items, and, on the benefit side, consumer surplus and profitability. In spite of these differences, however, there is considerable overlap between the two concepts.

As Mansfield points out, his estimates may be low because in every case where there was a choice, he consistently took the assumption that would yield lower rather than higher estimates of returns to innovation expenditure. The median direct rate of return to the innovating firm of 25 percent is very similar to the return estimated by the author and by Griliches for the direct returns. However, the implied indirect return, i.e., the difference between the two medians, of 30 percent is considerably lower than the 80 percent return calculated by the author. It is possible that the conservative assumptions taken by Mansfield, the difference in concepts or the difference in coverage explain the difference between the two estimates and that the 80 percent indirect productivity return estimated by the author through the interindustry regression equation is a good estimate of the actual indirect returns. However, it is also possible that the vintage effects correlated with R&D effects which could not be examined had inflated the magnitude of the indirect effects estimated by the author; or it is possible that the shortcomings of the measurement used by the author for human capital had a similar effect and that the external return was much lower, perhaps close to the 30 percent.

Because considerable uncertainty exists regarding the magnitude of the indirect returns at the present state of economic research, alternative estimates are calculated in the next section. Two different series are computed, each based on the economy-wide research intensity ratio. One version uses the author's coefficients of return to privately financed R&D, of 30 and 80 percent, respectively, for the direct and indirect returns. In the other, Mansfield's rates of return of 25 and 30 percent are introduced as coefficients in the same estimating equation.

Measuring the Possible Effect of R&D on Economic Growth

The direct ratio of internal R&D to value added for company financed R&D in the aggregate for all the 33 industries included in the author's study was 1.2 percent in the base year 1958. Using the estimate of a 30 percent rate of return, the component of growth in productivity (and hence in output) of these industries attributable to direct R&D may be calculated as 0.3 of 1.2 percent, or 0.36 percent. This corresponds to about one-eighth of the rate of productivity growth in the 33 industries, which was 2.8 percent a year.

The rate of productivity return on indirect R&D, estimated at 80 percent, is more than 2.5 times higher than the rate of direct return. But not all the R&D conducted in the 33 industries can be attributed to these industries on the basis of their sales. The absolute amount of total company financed R&D "purchased" by the 33 industries is reduced by 40 percent through sales outside these industries, i.e., sales to other industries, government, households, and abroad. Therefore, the ratio of purchased R&D to value added in the 33 industries is 0.72 percent (0.6 times 1.2 percent) in the base year. Correspondingly, an 80 percent productivity return to purchased R&D would suggest that 0.58 percent per year in productivity growth of the industries studied could be attributed to the indirect or externality effects of the R&D as transmitted through purchases.

The two components, direct and indirect, add up to a total growth effect of 0.9 percent (0.94) a year for the 33 industries studied, which is one-third (33 percent) of the growth of total factor productivity of these industries during this period and 23 percent of the rate of growth of their output, which grew at 4.0 percent.

The 33 industries for which these estimates are made include most of the manufacturing, mining, agricultural, utility and transportation industries. The total value added in these industries represented 69 percent of the private domestic economy and 58 percent of GNP in the base year 1958.

The extrapolation of the estimated effects to the entire economy involves comparisons with the corresponding growth rates in the private domestic economy and in GNP. Because the sectors of the economy not included among the 33 industries had smaller growth in output and productivity than did these industries, the relative significance of the contribution of R&D to economic growth is reduced less than in proportion to the share of the value added of the 33 industries in GNP and in the private domestic economy.

In considering the total economic growth effect of R&D, an upward adjustment is made in the intensity ratio for the 25 percent of private industrial R&D sold to industries other than the 33 industries included in the study. It is assumed that the output and productivity effects are being measured in those industries. No adjustments need to be made for the R&D sold to government, households or abroad because whatever its real effects may be, they would not appear in the measured growth under the existing statistical definitions. With this adjustment for the other industries, the ratio of purchased R&D to value added is 0.7 percent ($1.2 \times .85 \times .69$) for the private domestic economy and 0.6 percent for GNP. Assuming that the indirect rate of productivity return of 80 percent estimated within the manufacturing industries also applies to other sectors, these indirect effects would contribute 0.56 percent and 0.48 percent to the annual growth of productivity in the private economy and in the national economy (Net National Product), respectively. At the same time, the direct effects would contribute 0.21 percent and 0.18 percent, respectively, totalling 0.77 and 0.66 percent. The total growth rates of the residual for the private economy and for the national economy during the period 1948-66 were 2.5 and 2.3 percent; the output growth was 4.0 and 4.1 percent, respectively.[10]

The derivations for the period 1948-66 can be summarized as follows:

	Private Domestic Economy	GNP
Growth in output	4.0	4.1
Growth in total factor productivity ("residual")	2.5	2.3
Productivity growth attributed to R&D	0.8	0.7

This may be a somewhat low estimate of the entire economic growth effect of the national total of all R&D activities because it does not include any allowance for possible indirect or spillover effects from government financed R&D. (The reason is that no stable estimate could be obtained for such effects in nonmanufacturing, where they appear to exist.) Nor does it include any estimates of the (largely indirect) economic growth effects of the R&D performed in government, universities or nonprofit institutions, whether government or privately financed. In addition, an indicated in the author's earlier study,[11] the present estimates of the productivity returns to R&D may also be too low because they are statistically imputed to the estimates of gross investment rather than net investment in R&D. On the other hand, present estimates may be too high if they include components which should be attributed either to increases in human capital or to "vintage" improvements in physical capital not related to R&D, complementary to increases in R&D capital, but not included in the estimating equations.

One may extend this analysis a step further and construct annual estimates of economic growth attributable to industrial R&D by assuming that the productivity rates of return to R&D, which were estimated as averages applicable to the entire period of analysis (1948-66), also apply to individual years during the period and to some years after it. At the cost of making those assumptions, one gains the opportunity to trace the implications of changes in the R&D intensity of the economy which, in turn, results from changes in the levels of R&D investments and of economic activity.

Changes in the research intensity of the economy have been considerable over the past 20 years, as can be seen in Chart 6-1 graphically, and from the data in Table 6-4. The measure of research intensity shown is the ratio of the privately financed industrial R&D as a percent of the business gross product. Business gross product currently represents 96 percent of all private output in the United States (it excludes production by households and by nonprofit institutions) and 84 percent of GNP.

In line with the preceding discussion of the results of economic research on the effects of industrial R&D on economic growth, only the private expenditure for industrial R&D is included in the

CHART 6-1
PRIVATELY FINANCED INDUSTRIAL RESEARCH AND DEVELOPMENT AS A PERCENT OF BUSINESS GROSS PRODUCT IN THE UNITED STATES, 1953-73

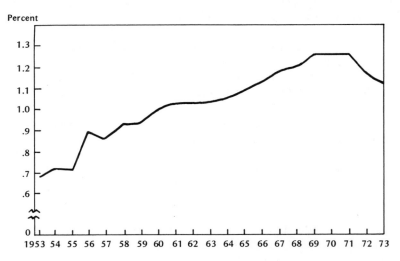

Source: See Table 6-4.

TABLE 6-4

PRIVATELY FINANCED INDUSTRIAL RESEARCH AND
DEVELOPMENT AS A PERCENT OF BUSINESS GROSS
PRODUCT IN THE UNITED STATES, 1953-73

Year	Percent	Year	Percent
1953	.69	1964	1.07
1954	.73	1965	1.10
1955	.71	1966	1.13
1956	.90	1967	1.19
1957	.89	1968	1.22
1958	.94	1969	1.26
1959	.95	1970	1.26
1960	1.02	1971	1.26
1961	1.05	1972	1.17
1962	1.05	1973	1.13
1963	1.06		

SOURCES

For research and development expenditure: National Science Foundation, National Patterns of R&D Resources, Funds and Manpower in the United States, 1953-1974, NSF-74-304 (Washington, D.C., February 1974), Table B-5. For business gross product: Executive Office of the President, Council of Economic Advisers, Economic Report of the President (Washington, D.C: U.S. Government Printing Office, 1974), Table C-9, p. 260.

numerator of the R&D intensity ratio because, as indicated earlier, no reliable indication was obtained that government financed industrial R&D, or other components of national R&D activity, have measurable effects on economic productivity, at least within the existing economic accounting and measurement framework for output, input and productivity.

Having obtained the time series for the R&D intensity of the economy, it is a relatively simple matter to calculate the economic growth effects of industrial R&D using the rate of return coefficients for direct and indirect effects.

The calculation is made by the relevant part of the formula for the estimating equation discussed above, i.e.:

$$\hat{p} = b_1 I_1 + b_2 I_2$$

where p is that part of the annual productivity growth rate attributed to R&D investments, I_1 is the research intensity ratio of the business gross product for the privately financed R&D conducted in the business sector, which was shown in Table 6-4, I_2 is the R&D intensity ratio for the privately financed R&D "sold" (i.e., attributed by sales) in the private sector (which is 85 percent of all privately financed R&D as redistributed by the 1958 input-output matrixes), and $b_1 = .3$, $b_2 = .8$, as estimated in the author's study. No time lag is allowed in this initial calculation between R&D and productivity change. Thus, the formula becomes

$$p_t = b_1 I_{1t} + b_2 (.85\ I_{1t})$$

where the subscript t refers to the given calendar year. The productivity growth rate calculated by this formula, using the author's values of $b_1 = .3$ and $b_2 = .8$ and the values of I_t from Table 6-4, is shown in Table 6-5. Also shown in the table is the corresponding estimate of productivity growth calculated using Mansfield's estimates of $b_1 = .25$ and $b_2 = .3$.

TABLE 6-5

ANNUAL RATE OF PRODUCTIVITY GROWTH IN THE
BUSINESS GROSS PRODUCT ATTRIBUTED TO INDUSTRIAL
R&D UNDER DIFFERENT ASSUMPTIONS ABOUT THE
MAGNITUDE OF DIRECT AND INDIRECT RETURNS
(Percent)

Year	Indirect Returns at 80% Direct Returns at 30%	Indirect Returns at 30% Direct Returns at 25%
1953	.66	.34
1954	.71	.36
1955	.69	.36
1956	.86	.44
1957	.86	.44
1958	.91	.47
1959	.91	.48
1960	.98	.51
1961	1.01	.52
1962	1.01	.52
1963	1.02	.53
1964	1.04	.54
1965	1.07	.55
1966	1.10	.57
1967	1.15	.60
1968	1.18	.61
1969	1.23	.63
1970	1.23	.63
1971	1.18	.61
1972	1.13	.58
1973	1.08	.56

Sources: Nestor E. Terleckyj, Effects of R&D on the Productivity Growth of
Industries: An Exploratory Study (Washington, D.C.: National Planning Association, 1974), pp. 43–45; Edwin Mansfield, John Rapoport, Anthony Romeo,
Samuel Wagner, George Beardsley, Social and Private Rates of Return from Industrial Innovation, University of Pennsylvania, preliminary and unpublished, 1975
(to appear in a forthcoming issue of the Quarterly Journal of Economics).

In the final step of estimation, the percentage growth from Table
6-5 is applied to the actual constant dollar amount of the business
gross product for the respective year to calculate the dollar value
of the measurable economic growth attributed to industrial
R&D.[12] The results of this calculation are shown in Table 6-6 and
Chart 6-2. In both, the two sets of estimates of the productivity
returns are used, the author's and Mansfield's. The growth
increment attributed to R&D that was calculated using the
author's estimates of the R&D effects is twice as large as that
calculated with coefficients based on Mansfield's results. In the
1970s, the two respective increments amount to about $12 billion
and $6 billion a year. The relative time pattern of the two sets of
changes is the same, since both were derived from the same R&D

TABLE 6-6

VALUE OF ECONOMIC GROWTH ATTRIBUTED TO PRODUCTIVITY
EFFECTS OF INDUSTRIAL R&D. TWO SETS OF ESTIMATES OF
DIRECT AND INDIRECT PRODUCTIVITY EFFECTS ON BUSINESS
GROSS PRODUCT, 1953-73
(Billions of 1973 dollars)

Year	Direct effects: 30% Indirect effects: 80%	Direct effects: 25% Indirect effects: 30%
1953	$3.5	$1.8
1954	3.7	1.9
1955	3.8	2.0
1956	4.9	2.5
1957	5.0	2.5
1958	5.2	2.7
1959	5.6	2.9
1960	6.1	3.2
1961	6.4	3.3
1962	6.9	3.5
1963	7.2	3.8
1964	7.8	4.0
1965	8.5	4.4
1966	9.2	4.8
1967	10.0	5.2
1968	10.7	5.6
1969	11.5	5.9
1970	11.4	5.9
1971	11.2	5.8
1972	11.6	6.0
1973	11.8	6.1

Source: See Table 6-5.

intensity ratio and the business gross product data. These estimates suggest that the amount of production attributable to R&D
grew rapidly in the 1950s and '60s but remained level in the '70s.

Regarding their time dimension, the estimates may be interpreted to indicate the potential net value of output attributed to R&D
conducted during the given year, calculated on the basis of an
average relationship derived from the statistics for a base period.[13] The time when this output is produced is not shown by this
indicator.

Over a long enough period, the underlying average relationship
can be estimated from aggregated data, such as those used by

CHART 6-2

VALUE OF ECONOMIC GROWTH ATTRIBUTED TO PRODUCTIVITY EFFECTS OF INDUSTRIAL R&D. TWO SETS OF ESTIMATES OF DIRECT AND INDIRECT PRODUCTIVITY EFFECTS ON BUSINESS GROSS PRODUCT, 1953-73 (in 1973 dollars)

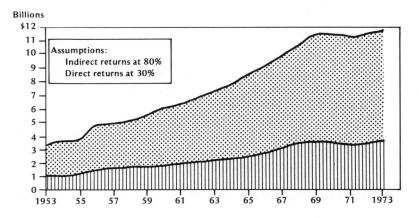

Billions

Assumptions:
Indirect returns at 80%
Direct returns at 30%

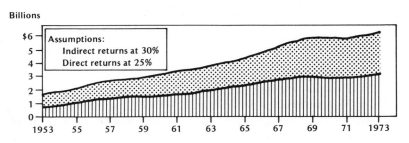

Billions

Assumptions:
Indirect returns at 30%
Direct returns at 25%

Source: See Table 6-6.

the author. This relationship, as indicated earlier, estimates the net return to R&D approximating statistically the mean internal rate of productivity return[14] on the R&D expenditures made during the period, provided the period is long enough to encompass a large number of complete cost and return life cycles of the individual R&D projects relative to the number (amount) of incomplete cycles reflected in the data for the period. The 18-year period used by the author should be suffi-

143

ciently long to derive estimates of such returns since the bulk of cost and payoff of R&D projects occurs within 6- to 10-year periods.

However, the actual returns to R&D expenditure made during a given year occur over the years, with the bulk following the expenditure by a number of years. Mansfield's study provides for the first time much information on the timing, dispersion, incidence and possible time trends of returns to R&D.

It is not practical within the scope of this essay to attempt a synthesis of aggregate cross-section estimates and microlevel time series results which might lead to development of a more sophisticated (distributed lag) time series indicator than the one shown in the preceding chart. Another subject which has to be deferred to a future study is consideration of the possible depreciation of industrial R&D and its effect on the estimates of growth attributable to R&D.

In conclusion, it should be noted again that the indicators estimating the effects of industrial R&D on economic growth constructed here are quite experimental and subject to change in the light of future findings. Nevertheless, they do reflect the present state of economic knowledge and suggest a format in which this knowledge can be organized.

Notes

1 For a summary, see the symposium papers in the National Science Foundation, *Research and Development and Economic Growth/Productivity,* Papers and Proceedings of a Colloquium (NSF 72-303), (Washington, D.C.: U.S. Government Printing Office, 1972) and individual studies cited in it and in National Science Board, *Science Indicators 1974* (Washington, D.C.: U.S. Government Printing Office, 1975), p. 110-112.

2 See Nestor E. Terleckyj, *Effects of R&D on the Productivity Growth of Industries: An Exploratory Study* (Washington, D.C.: National Planning Association, 1974) and "Direct and Indirect Effects of Industrial Research and Development on the Productivity Growth of Industries," paper given at the November 1975 Conference on Research in Income and Wealth, to appear

in a forthcoming volume, *New Developments in Productivity Measurement,* published by the National Bureau of Economic Research in the series of volumes of the conference on Research in Income and Wealth.

3 Zvi Griliches, "Research Expenditures and Growth Accounting," *Science and Technology in Economic Growth,* ed. B.R. Williams, Proceedings of a Conference held by the International Economic Association at St. Anton, Austria (New York: John Wiley & Sons, Halsted Press, 1973), pp. 61-65; and Terleckyj, *Effects of R&D,* pp. 3-7.

4 John W. Kendrick, *Postwar Productivity Trends in the United States, 1948-1969* (New York: National Bureau of Economic Research, 1973).

5 Murray Brown and Alfred H. Conrad, "The Influence of Research and Education on CES Production Relations," *The Theory and Empirical Analysis of Production,* ed. Murray Brown, Studies in Income and Wealth No. 31 (New York: National Bureau of Economic Research, 1967); and Fredric Q. Raines, "The Impact of Applied Research and Development on Productivity," paper read at the Southern Economic Association Meeting, Washington, D.C., November 1968.

6 In the course of research, other R&D intensity ratios were considered, e.g., for all direct R&D (privately and government financed). In the end, the fourfold division of R&D was accepted because different results were obtained for each of the four R&D components shown in Table 6-2.

7 Nestor E. Terleckyj, "Sources of Productivity Advance: A Pilot Study of Manufacturing Industries 1899-1953," Ph.D dissertation, Columbia University, 1960, pp. 83, 105-106.

8 Zvi Griliches, "Returns to Research and Development Expenditures in the Private Sector," paper given at the November 1975 Conference on Research in Income and Wealth, to appear in a forthcoming volume *New Developments in Productivity Measurement,* and Griliches, "Research Expenditures and Growth Accounting."

9 Edwin Mansfield, John Rapoport, Anthony Romeo, Samuel

Wagner and George Beardsley, *Social and Private Rates of Return from Industrial Innovation,* University of Pennsylvania, preliminary and unpublished, 1975 (to appear in a forthcoming issue of the *Quarterly Journal of Economics*).

10 Kendrick, *Postwar Productivity Trends,* pp. 138-143.

11 Terleckyj, *Effects of R&D on Productivity Growth of Industries,* pp. 6-8.

12 Growth attributed in the business sector is the total economic growth which can be so attributed. The growth effects of R&D in the remaining producing sectors of the economy, representing 16 percent of GNP, are not measurable at present.

13 Here 1948-66; Mansfield's data apply to the period from 1960 to the present and include in part some projections to 1980.

14 The term "internal" rate of return used here is the technical expression designating the mathematical formula used in computing the return (i.e., interest or yield) from given time series of costs and returns. It is to be distinguished from the returns to internal or own R&D and R&D attributed or purchased from other industries estimated by the author. Mathematically, both of those rates are "internal."

7 Medical Advances and Life Expectancy, 1940-70

Joseph Schachter

Introduction

The past several decades have been notable for substantial public investment in biomedical research and development, and for a number of significant advances in disease prevention, diagnosis and therapy. In recent years, however, funds earmarked for this purpose have leveled off, and the demand for accountability in terms of end results has become more insistent. At the same time, sharply rising costs of health service delivery have stimulated competition for federal allocations in the health field. This has been compounded by the dilemma that medical discoveries not infrequently spell higher costs of health care. As the number of available laboratory tests has grown, so has the pressure on the physician to utilize them.

While many health scientists believe that their research achievements speak for themselves, others have attempted to justify the costs in terms of resulting economic benefits.[1] These include the direct savings in physician services, drugs and hospitalization, and the indirect monetary gains from the reduction of work loss due to morbidity and mortality. There are also the intangible benefits of diminished pain, suffering and anxiety.

The consequences of advances in the field of medicine are profound and far-reaching. They encompass the methods of financing health care, medical education and licensure; the specialization of medicine, the ways in which physicians have organized their practice, the number and types of paramedical personnel, the manner in which services are provided, the size and composition of the population. A comprehensive discussion of the manifold primary and secondary effects of recent medical advances is beyond the scope of this chapter. It will be limited to a consideration of the impact on life expectancy in the United States and the methodological problems incident to such an assessment.

Selection of Discoveries for Analysis

Since limited resources precluded the preparation of life table computations for every discovery of modern medicine, a process of selection became necessary. For this purpose, four criteria were developed.

(1) The discovery was introduced in the United States since 1940.
(2) It resulted in a significant reduction in mortality or provided immunity against a seriously crippling disease.
(3) The cause (or causes) of death affected are identified in the official vital statistics tabulations both currently and in the year immediately preceding the discovery's introduction.
(4) Relative to the causes, measures exist which permit determination of the comparability of the data over time.

As the data were examined, it became clear that few discoveries completely fulfilled all the requirements. The process of selection began with a review of published articles concerning recent health science advances. The discoveries singled out for mention differed, depending on the author's focus. Wain, for example, limited himself to developments in preventive medicine.[2] Fudenberg, LeSourd and others were concerned with discoveries which produced fiscal returns through their direct and indirect economic benefits.[3] Frequently, such benefits were realized primarily through reduction in morbidity. Burch discussed medical advances in relation to downward trends in mortality from specified causes.[4] A report meriting special attention was prepared by the American Medical Association in 1964, portions of which are reproduced in Appendix A to this chapter.[5] The work is based on a survey of physicians in the various medical specialties who were asked to name recent medical discoveries they would least want to forego.

After careful consideration, and with some relaxation of the criteria, six discoveries were selected for analysis. This selection may be biased against more recent advances because of the time lag between a discovery and its public recognition. The discoveries are listed in Table 7-1, together with the year in which each was "introduced." In point of fact, a medical discovery ordinarily is adopted over a period of time, and it is difficult to designate a calendar year during which it came into general use, if indeed this state was ever reached. Penicillin was discovered in 1928 by Sir Alexander Fleming, but it was not until World War II that it was applied, first in the military population, and then, as supplies became available, in the civilian population.[6]

TABLE 7-1

SELECTED MEDICAL DISCOVERIES AND DISEASES AFFECTED

Discovery	Year Introduced	Disease Affected
Penicillin	1943	Pneumonia, syphilis, rheumatic fever and rheumatic heart disease, appendicitis
Salk Vaccine	1955	Poliomyelitis
Hydralazine	1950	Hypertension and hypertensive heart disease
Pap Smear Test	1943	Uterine cancer
Streptomycin	1944	Tuberculosis
Transplantation Technology	1962	Chronic nephritis, renal sclerosis, and chronic pyelonephritis

The Salk vaccine's relationship to poliomyelitis is straightforward, and there were no statistical or classificational problems in measuring its effect. Polio did not, however, cause many deaths. During 1950-54, the annual death rate from this disease averaged only 1.3 per 100,000 population, compared with the overall total of 954.0 per 100,000.[7] Poliomyelitis was a dread disease for a combination of reasons: its victims were primarily children, it was sometimes lethal, it often seriously crippled for life, and it could strike anywhere and at any time.

Nature and Sources of Data

The age-sex specific mortality rates in Appendix B to this chapter are based on published and unpublished data from the National Center for Health Statistics. Deaths are tabulated according to the "International Classification of Diseases," sometimes referred to as the "International Lists." This system is revised every 10 years to update the disease terms in keeping with advances in medical science and changes in diagnostic practice. The periodic revisions are numbered, and the one currently in effect (1968-77) is the eighth.[8]

A first step in developing the data base was to identify the rubrics in the present revision for the diseases in question, and then find matching categories in the revisions applicable prior to the discoveries. Unfortunately for time series analysis, the decennial revisions often introduce discontinuities in the rates. This is compounded by concomitant changes in the rules for selecting the underlying cause of death. As a result, it was not always feasible to obtain statistics for a prior year with which valid comparisons could be made. A number of examples are cited.

RH hemolytic disease (erythroblastosis fetalis) was a disorder of obscure etiology prior to the discovery in 1940 of the RH blood factor by Landsteiner and Weiner.[9] In the fifth revision, then in effect, it was lumped with "other diseases of the newborn." Not until 1949, with the application of the sixth revision, were RH factor deaths separately counted.

Another discovery considered for study but subsequently omitted because of overriding statistical problems was the internal electronic cardiac pacemaker. It was introduced in 1958, and by 1972 an estimated 120,000 devices had been surgically implanted in patients with heart block.[10] This is a condition in which the signal generated by the heart's natural pacemaker does not reach the lower pumping chambers due to disruption of the conduction system. As a consequence, the ventricles beat independently of the atria, and generally at a much slower rate. The reduced cardiac output may lead to Stokes-Adams seizures and other complications. The artificial pacemaker provides an electrical impulse to stimulate contraction of ventricles at an adequate rate.

An important difficulty in measuring the impact of this discovery is in the diagnosis of heart block as the cause of death. In the living, this disease can be detected by electrocardiography. Once death has occurred, however, it is virtually impossible to diagnose. Hence, in the absence of a clinical history, death could well be attributed to ischemic heart disease. Another problem is to identify the proper category in the International Lists. In the eighth revision there is none exclusively for heart block.

The third example is cancer of the cervix uteri, a disease detected with the Pap smear. Unfortunately, in the 1942 classification of deaths, distinctions were not made to delineate this type of uterine cancer. It was decided to include the discovery nonetheless, but to measure its impact in terms of changes in the death rate for cancer of the uterus. In effect, it is assumed that among such cancers, the proportion endometrial is substantially constant over time.

To allow correction for the disjunction in statistical trends due to revisions in the International Lists and in the coding rules, comparability ratios were developed. They are based on data obtained by dual coding; i.e., coding cause of death in accordance with each of the two revisions in question, using the same set of death certificates.[11] A measure is then obtained by dividing the gross count of the more recent revision by that of the earlier. To the extent that the ratio varies from unity, it indicates the net relative amount gained or lost by each title through the introduction of the revised classification. A single ratio for a disease group was applied to each of the age-sex subgroups, since more detailed factors were not generally available or had large sampling errors.

Life Table Preparation and Results

The figures obtained were forwarded to the Office of the Actuary, Social Security Administration, where the life tables were prepared. From the mass of detail provided, certain figures on expectation of life were abstracted for presentation in Table 7-2. They indicate what the average remaining lifetime would have been in 1970 had the death rates for certain causes remained at the levels that prevailed before the six medical discoveries. Also shown is the difference in years between this set of figures and those based on the actual 1970 mortality experience. These statistics are displayed for four points in time: at birth, at age 20, at age 40, and at age 65. If the nine causes are taken together at their earlier levels, life expectancy at birth would have been 68.6 years, compared with the actual figure of 70.9 years. In other words, given the assumptions inherent in this model, the discoveries translate to a net gain of 2.3 years of life.

The average remaining lifetime is computed from life table statistics by dividing the total number of man-years lived by a cohort subsequent to a specified exact age by the number in the cohort living to the exact age. Obviously, a reduction of given

TABLE 7-2
HYPOTHETICAL LIFE EXPECTANCY ASSUMING 1970 MORTALITY AS MODIFIED BY THE SUBSTITUTION OF EARLIER (HIGHER) RATES FOR SPECIFIED CAUSES, AND DIFFERENCES FROM LIFE EXPECTANCY BASED ENTIRELY ON 1970 MORTALITY*

Disease Group	Hypothetical Life Expectancy and Difference from 1970 Actual							
	At Birth		At Age 20		At Age 40		At Age 65	
	Hypo-thetical	Diff.	Hypo-thetical	Diff.	Hypo-thetical	Diff.	Hypo-thetical	Diff.
All Listed Diseases Combined	68.56	2.32	51.39	1.78	33.43	1.23	14.44	0.63
Tuberculosis	70.08	0.80	52.47	0.70	34.32	0.34	14.99	0.08
Pneumonia	70.35	0.53	52.98	0.19	34.52	0.14	14.99	0.08
Hypertension & Hypertensive Heart Disease	70.55	0.33	52.82	0.35	34.32	0.34	14.80	0.27
Rheumatic Fever & Rheumatic Heart Disease	70.56	0.32	52.90	0.27	34.47	0.19	14.94	0.13
Uterine Cancer	70.73	0.15	53.01	0.16	34.53	0.13	15.03	0.04
Appendicitis	70.76	0.12	53.09	0.08	34.62	0.04	15.06	0.01
Syphilis	70.83	0.05	53.12	0.05	34.62	0.04	15.06	0.01
Chronic Nephritis, Renal Sclerosis, & Chronic Pyelonephritis	70.83	0.05	53.12	0.05	34.63	0.03	15.05	0.02
Poliomyelitis	70.85	0.03	53.16	0.01	34.66	0.00	15.07	0.00

*1970 Actual Life Expectancy: At Birth 70.88; at Age 20 53.17; at Age 40 34.66; at Age 65 15.07.

Source: Office of the Actuary, Social Security Administration, HEW. Life Tables prepared specifically for this study.

magnitude in the mortality rate will have a greater effect on life expectation when it occurs early in the lifespan of the cohort. The size of the cohort is then larger, and more lives are saved at a given rate. Also, each survivor contributes for a longer time to the total man-years lived, all other things being equal.

As would be expected, causes having low death rates to begin with could be virtually eliminated without any appreciable effect on average length of life. The reduction in poliomyelitis, with a prior death rate of about 1 per 100,000, contributed an insignificant 0.03 years of life. Even the largest contribution, made by the reduction in the death rate for tuberculosis, was only 0.80 years.

Discussion

A critical feature of this analysis is the implied cause and effect relationship between the medical discovery and the downward trend in mortality for the disease category to which it relates. While it is reasonable to surmise that the discovery contributed to the decline, other factors were obviously involved. Frequently, the drop in mortality started some time before the discovery was introduced. To provide some historical perspective, the trends in mortality for the nine cause groups are shown in Chart 7-1. The data were plotted without adjustment, and the discontinuities resulting from decennial revisions in classification are sometimes apparent. This graph also serves to illustrate that downturns in mortality often antedate the discoveries credited. These data are also listed in Table 7-3.

Improved standards of living and higher educational levels have contributed substantially to the betterment of health status in the United States. The reduced rates of mortality also reflect the latent effect of earlier discoveries, as well as the benefits of recent medical advances not included among the six selected for study. Table 7-7, which recapitulates the principal data of this report, lists a number of other relevant discoveries.

It is useful to view the estimated gains against the background of life expectancy trends since 1930. The figures in Table 7-4, taken from official life tables,[12] reflect the death rates from all causes in the contemporary year. The largest gain occurred between 1940

CHART 7-1
DEATH RATES FOR SPECIFIED CAUSES OF DEATH, UNITED STATES, 1940-73 (deaths per 100,000 population)

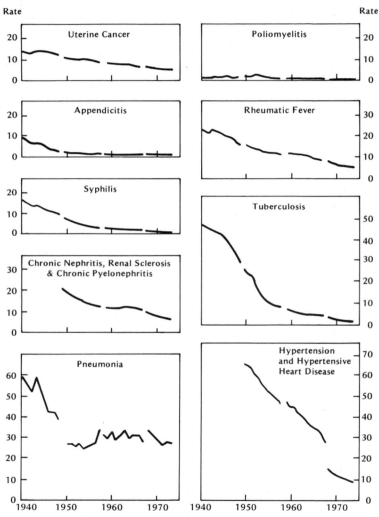

Note: Data not adjusted for revisions in international classification of diseases effective in 1949, 1958 and 1968.

Source: See Table 7-3.

TABLE 7-3

DEATH RATES FOR SPECIFIED CAUSES OF DEATH, UNITED STATES, 1940-73
(Deaths per 100,000 Population)

Year	Appendi-citis	Uterine Cancer	Polio	Rheu-matic Fever	Chronic Nephri-tis, etc.	Syphilis	Hyper-tension, etc.	Pneu-monia	Tuber-culosis
1973	0.5	5.6	0.0	6.5	6.1	0.2	9.6	27.4	1.8
1972	0.6	5.8	0.0	6.8	6.7	0.2	10.2	27.7	2.1
1971	0.6	5.9	0.1	7.1	7.1	0.2	10.6	27.0	2.2
1970	0.7	5.9	0.1	7.3	7.7	0.2	11.4	29.0	2.6
1969	0.7	6.1	0.1	7.6	8.3	0.3	12.2	30.9	2.8
1968	0.7	6.4	0.1	8.2	8.7	0.3	13.4	33.2	3.1
1967	0.8	6.6	0.1	7.2	9.6	1.2	30.9	28.0	3.5
1966	0.8	6.8	0.1	7.7	10.1	1.1	33.5	31.0	3.9
1965	0.9	7.1	0.1	8.0	10.5	1.3	34.4	30.8	4.1
1964	0.9	7.3	0.1	8.3	11.0	1.4	36.4	30.2	4.3
1963	0.9	7.5	0.1	8.8	10.7	1.4	39.1	33.8	4.3
1962	1.0	7.7	0.1	9.5	10.8	1.5	40.1	30.4	5.1
1961	1.0	7.9	0.1	9.8	10.8	1.6	41.3	29.0	5.4
1960	1.0	8.0	0.2	10.3	11.0	1.6	44.1	32.9	6.1
1959	1.0	8.1	0.4	10.4	10.9	1.7	46.0	29.6	6.5
1958	1.1	8.7	0.2	10.8	12.0	2.0	50.7	30.6	7.1
1957	1.2	8.7	0.2	11.8	12.5	2.2	49.0	31.4	7.8
1956	1.3	8.8	0.4	12.0	12.5	2.3	49.8	26.8	8.4
1955	1.4	9.3	0.7	12.0	12.6	2.3	51.8	25.4	9.1
1954	1.4	9.4	0.9	12.1	13.3	3.0	53.7	23.8	10.2
1953	1.5	9.8	1.0	13.3	14.5	3.3	59.1	27.0	12.4
1952	1.7	9.8	2.1	13.7	15.7	3.7	61.9	26.1	15.8
1951	1.9	10.0	1.1	14.1	16.8	4.1	64.2	26.9	20.1
1950	2.0	10.6	1.4	14.8	18.5	5.0	64.8	26.9	22.5
1949	2.5	10.9	1.8	15.3	19.5	5.8	64.6	26.9	26.3
1948	2.9	11.7	1.3	16.6	NA	8.0	NA	35.2	30.0
1947	3.3	12.2	0.4	17.4	NA	8.8	NA	37.8	33.5
1946	3.8	12.3	1.3	17.6	NA	9.3	NA	38.3	36.4
1945	5.1	13.0	0.9	19.7	NA	10.6	NA	43.9	39.9
1944	5.9	12.9	1.0	20.3	NA	11.2	NA	48.5	41.2
1943	6.0	12.6	0.9	21.4	NA	12.1	NA	54.3	42.5
1942	6.2	12.2	0.4	20.0	NA	12.2	NA	47.5	43.1
1941	8.1	12.4	0.6	21.0	NA	13.3	NA	48.0	44.5
1940	9.9	12.7	0.8	22.1	NA	14.4	NA	54.9	45.9

NOTE: Data not adjusted for revisions in international classification of diseases effective in 1949, 1958 and 1968.

Source: U.S. National Center for Health Statistics.

and 1950, when life expectancy increased by 5.3 years. In the 1960-70 interval, the corresponding increase was only 1.2 years. There are several reasons why the impact of a medical discovery may not be fully reflected in the selected underlying cause of death. This study attempted to consider only the principal diseases affected; there may well be others which were favorably influenced by the discovery. Another factor is the method of assigning a death to a single cause. When several contributing causes are listed on the death certificate, the death is assigned to the underlying cause. A patient hospitalized for a fractured pelvis

TABLE 7-4

EXPECTATION OF LIFE AT BIRTH FOR SELECTED YEARS:
UNITED STATES, 1930-70

Calendar Year	Remaining Years of Life	Change Decennially (in years)
1970	70.9	1.2
1960	69.7	1.5
1950	68.2	5.3
1940	62.9	3.2
1930	59.7	--

Source: Vital Statistics of the United States, 1970, Volume II, Section 5.

who develops and then dies from pneumonia while bed ridden, would not, according to the rules, be tabulated as pneumonia death. This would be regarded as the immediate cause. The underlying, or antecedent, cause is the initial factor, e.g., the bone fracture, in the chain of events leading to death.[13] This points up an inherent limitation of the single-cause classification system. A large proportion of death certificates report two or more diseases or conditions as relevant etiology.[14] The coding for multiple causes would reflect the circumstances of death more realistically, and this has been done occasionally. However, no time series is available to satisfy the purposes of this study. A more basic consideration is the validity of the diagnostic information given on the death record. A number of studies have been made in this regard, and the findings suggest that the quality varies considerably, depending on the cause of death.[15]

Often, the full potential of a discovery to prevent death is not realized because of failure to take advantage of it. Surveys have found that substantial portions of a population are not availing themselves of modern medical procedures even though many years have elapsed since their introduction. According to a recent report by the National Center for Health Statistics, about one woman in four has never had a Pap smear test, and less than one-half have had the test during the past 12 months.[16] With regard to hypertension, recent studies have shown that about 40 percent of those with the condition were unaware of it, and of those who knew they were hypertensive, only about half were under proper medical control.[17]

Conclusion

Notwithstanding important medical advances in recent years, the average length of life has not increased dramatically. A factor which dampens the effect of a reduction in the death rate from one cause is the competing risk of dying from another.[18] Of greater significance is that there has been no discovery which has markedly reduced mortality from the major killing diseases. These diseases are, and for a long time have been, heart disease, cancer and stroke. Together, they account for most of the deaths in the United States. Table 7-5 shows their age-adjusted rates back to 1950. The basic pattern is consistent over time, notwithstanding modest changes. Table 7-6 indicates the effect on life expectancy if deaths from these causes were reduced to zero.[19] The elimination of all deaths from malignant neoplasms would add only 2.27 years to the average lifespan, and the elimination of stroke deaths (vascular lesions) would add only 1.29 years. If deaths from cardio-vascular-renal diseases were reduced to zero, a sizable increase—10.9 years—would occur, provided the other death rates did not increase. These figures are based on 1959-61 mortality, but in view of the general stability of death rates for these causes during the past decade, there is little reason to expect appreciably different results if more recent data were employed.

TABLE 7-5

AGE-ADJUSTED DEATH RATES FOR ALL CAUSES COMBINED,
AND FOR THE THREE LEADING CAUSES: UNITED STATES,
1950-72

Cause of Death (By 8th Rev. List Numbers)	1972	1971	1970	1960	1950
All Causes	701.8	699.9	714.3	760*	840*
Diseases of the Heart (390-398,402,404,410-429)	249.3	250.1	253.6	286.2	307.6
Malignant Neoplasms (140-209)	130.7	129.7	129.9	125.8	125.4
Cerebrovascular Diseases (430-438)	65.0	65.2	66.3	79.7	88.8

*Data accurate to only two significant digits, as published.

Sources: Data for 1970-72, unpublished figures, NCHS (Mike Zugzda 1/22/75). Data for 1950 & 1960, all causes, Vital Statistics of the United States, 1969, Vol. II, Part A, Table 1-2. Data for 1950 & 1960, selected causes, Vital and Health Statistics Series 20, No. 16, PHS, NCHS.

157

TABLE 7-6

GAIN IN EXPECTATION OF LIFE AT BIRTH IF
SPECIFIED CAUSES OF DEATH WERE ELIMINATED,
UNITED STATES, 1959-61

Specified Cause (By 7th Revision List Numbers)	Gain in Years
Infective & Parasitic Diseases	.22
Tuberculosis	.10
Malignant Neoplasms	2.27
Diabetes	.22
Major Cardiovascular-Renal Diseases	10.90
Vascular Lesions Affecting Central Nervous System	1.29
Influenza & Pneumonia	.53

Source: "United States Life Tables by Cause of Death, 1959-61," PHS Publication No. 1252 (May 1968).

DISEASES TO WHICH THEY WERE APPLIED:
UNITED STATES, 1940-70

Disease Category and Classification Code (ICDA 8th Revision Codes)	Important Medical Advance	Approximate Time of Introduction	Other Relevant Medical Advances	Death Rates* per 100,000 Population		Estimate of Increased Life Expectancy at Birth (Years)*
				In Year Prior to Medical Advance Listed in Column (2)	In 1970	
(1)	(2)	(3)	(4)	(5)	(6)	(7)
Tuberculosis (010-019)	Streptomycin	1944	Isoniazid, para-amino salicylic acid, rifampin, ethambutol	38.8	2.6	.80
Poliomyelitis (040-044)	Salk vaccine	1955	Sabin vaccine	1.0	0.1	.03
Syphilis (090-097)	Penicillin	1943	Penicillin G procaine and G benzathine, tetracycline, erythromycin	2.9	0.2	.05
Cancer of the uterus (180-182)	Pap smear	1943	Radiological therapy, surgery, chemotherapy	11.6	5.9	.15
Rheumatic fever and rheumatic heart disease (390-398)	Penicillin	1943	Open heart surgery	21.9	7.3	.32
Hypertension and hypertensive heart disease (400-404)	Hydralazine	1950	Reserpine, thiazides, guanethidine, propranolol, methyldopa	30.7	11.4	.33
Pneumonia (480-486)	Penicillin	1943	Vaccines against influenza and pneumonia, tetramycin, erythromycin	40.3	29.0	.53
Appendicitis (540-543)	Penicillin	1943	Tetracycline, improved blood typing and storage, surgical and anesthesiologic progress	5.4	0.7	.12
Chronic nephritis, renal sclerosis and chronic pyelonephritis (582-584, 590)	Organ transplantation technology	1962	Dialysis, immunosuppressive therapy, histological matching, organ preservation, antibiotics	10.2	7.7	.05

* Rates for years prior to 1970 adjusted to 1970 basis to allow for revisions in coding rules and in decennial revisions of international classification of diseases. There is a difference in the estimate of increased life expectancy between the sum of the individual entries (2.38) and the estimate for the nine causes combined (2.32) which is due to interaction effects.

159

NOTES

1 Burton A. Weisbrod, *Econonics of Public Health* (Philadelphia: University of Pennsylvania Press, 1961); Herbert E. Klarman, *The Economics of Health* (New York: Columbia University Press, 1965); Dorothy P. Rice, "Estimating the Cost of Illness," Health Economic Series No. 6, Public Health Service Publication No. 947 (1966); and "Facts on the Major Killing and Crippling Diseases in the United States" (New York: The National Health Education Committee, Inc., 1971).

2 Harry Wain, *A History of Preventive Medicine* (Springfield, Ill.: Charles C. Thomas, 1970).

3 H. H. Fudenberg, "The Dollar Benefits of Biomedical Research: A Cost Analysis," *The Journal of Laboratory and Clinical Medicine,* Vol. 79, No. 3 (March 1972); Fudenberg, "Fiscal Returns of Biomedical Research," *The Journal of Investigative Dermatology,* No. 61, pp. 321-329 (1973); and David A. LeSourd, Mark E. Fogel and Donald R. Johnston, "Benefit/Cost Analysis of Kidney Disease Programs" (August 1968).

4 George E. Burch, *Contributions of the Biological Sciences to Human Welfare: Federation Proceedings,* Vol. 31, No. 6, Part II (November-December 1972), Chapter III, "Clinical Medicine."

5 Commission on the Cost of Medical Care, *Significant Medical Advances,* Vol. III (American Medical Association, 1964).

6 Wain, *A History of Preventive Medicine;* and William F. Marlow, Jr., "Syphilis Then and Now," *Journal of the American Medical Association,* Vol. 230, No. 9 (December 2, 1974).

7 Robert D. Grove and Alice M. Hetzel, "Vital Statistics Rates in the United States, 1940-1960" (U.S. Department of Health, Education, and Welfare, Public Health Service, National Center for Health Statistics, 1968), Public Health Service Publication No. 1677.

8 "Eighth Revision, International Classification of Diseases, Adapted for Use in the United States," Vol. 1, *Tabular List 1969,* Public Health Service Publication No. 1693.

9 Wain, *A History of Preventive Medicine.*

10 "Implantable Cardiac Pacemakers: Status Report and Resource Guideline," Report of the Inter-Society Commission for Heart Disease Resources, *The American Journal of Cardiology,* Vol. 34 (October 1, 1974).

11 Robert A. Israel and Joan A. Klebba, "A Preliminary Report on the Effect of Eighth Revision ICDA on Cause of Death Statistics," *American Journal of Public Health,* Vol. 59, No. 9 (September 1969); Mattie M. Faust and Alice B. Dolman, "Comparability of Mortality Statistics for the Sixth and Seventh Revisions: United States, 1958," *Vital Statistics Special Reports,* Vol. 51, No. 4 (March 1965); and Faust and Dolman, "Comparability of Mortality Statistics for the Fifth and Sixth Revisions: United States, 1950," *Vital Statistics,* Vol. 51, No. 2.

12 *Vital Statistics of the United States,* 1970, Vol. II, "Section 5: Life Tables" (U.S. Department of Health, Education, and Welfare, Public Health Service, Health Resources Administration, National Center for Health Statistics, 1974).

13 "Physician's Handbook on Medical Certification: Death, Fetal Death, and Birth" (U.S. Department of Health, Education, and Welfare, Public Health Service, National Center for Health Statistics, 1967), Public Health Service Publication No. 593-B; and "Medical Certification of Cause of Death: Instruction for Physicians," *WHO Bulletin of the World Health Organization,* Supplement 3 (1952).

14 *Vital Statistics of the United States,* "Supplement, Multiple Causes of Death—1965" (U.S. Department of Health, Education, and Welfare, Public Health Service, National Center for Health Statistics, 1965); and Harold F. Dorn, "Underlying and Contributory Causes of Death," *Study of Cancer and Other Chronic Diseases,* National Cancer Institute Monograph No. 19 (January 1966).

15 Harold F. Dorn and Joseph I. Horn, "The Reliability of Certificates of Death from Cancer," *American Journal of Hygiene,* Vol. 34 (1941); Iwao M. Moriyama, William S. Baum, William M. Haenszel and Berwyn F. Mattison, "Inquiry into Diagnostic Evidence Supporting Medical Certification of

Death," *American Journal of Public Health,* Vol. 48, No. 10 (October 1958); Philip A. Wolf, William B. Kannel, Patricia M. McNamara and Thomas R. Dawber, "Assessment of Death Certification of Stroke: The Framingham Study," Abstracts of Conference on CVD Epidemiology, Tampa, Florida, March 10-11, 1975, *CVD Epidemiology Newsletter* No. 18 (American Heart Association, January 1975); and Iwao M. Moriyama, Thomas R. Dawber and William B. Kannel, "Evaluation of Diagnostic Information Supporting Medical Certification of Deaths from Cardiovascular Disease," *Study of Cancer and Other Chronic Diseases.*

16 Mary Wilder, "Current Estimates from the Health Interview Survey, 1973," National Center for Health Statistics, Series 10, No. 95.

17 Jeremiah Stamler, "High Blood Pressure in the United States—An Overview of the Problem and the Challenge," National Conference on High Blood Pressure Education, U.S. Department of Health, Education, and Welfare Publication No. NIH 73-486 (January 1973).

18 T.N.E. Greville, "Mortality Tables Analyzed by Cause of Death" *The Record,* American Institute of Actuaries, Vol. XXXVII, Part II, No. 76 (October 1948).

19 Francisco Bayo, "United States Life Tables by Causes of Death: 1959- 61," Vol. 1, No. 6, Public Health Service Publication No. 1252 (May 1968).

Appendix A to Chapter 7: Significant Medical Advances

Appendix A, containing Volume III, *Significant Medical Advances*, by the Commission on the Cost of Medical Care (AMA, 1964), pp. ix, 3-17, is reproduced by permission of the American Medical Association.

INTRODUCTION

The past 25 years have witnessed a phenomenal expansion in medical science, as many new and revolutionary drugs and medical procedures were developed. This volume presents data relating to these medical advances and examines their consequence.

The initial step in this undertaking was the definition of what constitutes a *significant* advance, as it relates to the practice of medicine. Significance, in this instance, refers to that item or technique which the practicing physician would *least* want to forego.

Part I presents the results of the application of this criterion by physicians to developments in their special area of practice. For the first time, a list is presented showing what each specialty considers to be the most significant developments during the period 1936-1962 (Chapter 1). Consultants to the American Medical Association's Council on Drugs were used to develop a list of the most significant pharmaceuticals (Chapter 2).

In Part II, a methodology is developed (Chapter 3) for a more detailed analysis of five advances selected from Part I. In this framework, the development of the poliomyelitis vaccines (Chapter 4), the early detection of uterine cancer (Chapter 5), the surgical correction of congenital heart defects (Chapter 6), the introduction of antituberculosis drugs (Chapter 7), and the evolution and use of disposable products (Chapter 8) are analyzed not only as to their importance in medical care but also as to their economic and social significance.

These advances were selected because they illustrate that innovations may result in various types of improvements. Poliomyelitis vaccines prevent the contracting of the disease and may lead to its virtual elimination; early detection of uterine cancer increases the chances of survival; surgical correction of congenital heart defects saves lives which otherwise would be lost in youth; antituberculosis drugs enable more rapid recovery from this disease; and disposable products replace more costly procedures and prevent cross-infection.

The five advances also illustrate that the costs involved in utilizing an advance may differ. When mass production can be applied, the cost per patient may be relatively low. In those areas where the cost per patient is high, advances must be considered significant in terms of lives saved and improved health.

In Part III, an overview is presented showing how gross benefits, both medical and socioeconomic, have accrued to the American public from the results of many and varied scientific endeavors. Because precise measurements are extremely difficult, this part of the study presents only the general implications of advances in medical science.

Medical science does not seek major credit for the improvements in the health level during the past 25 years. Certainly, higher standards of living and higher educational levels have contributed substantially to the betterment of the health level in the United States. However, this study documents a virtual "explosion" of medical advances and describes the resultant socioeconomic impact.

The readily recognized and appreciated technological advances tend to overshadow other wide-scale changes brought about by these developments. Scientific medical advances have profoundly affected such factors as the financing of health care, medical education and licensure, specialization of medicine, the ways in which physicians have organized their practice, the number and types of paramedical personnel, the manner in which services are provided to the patient, and the size and composition of the population.

It is hoped that the present volume will bring about an understanding and appreciation of improvements in the quality of medical care. The Commission is cognizant that medical care prices have increased, but it is equally aware that medical services have greatly improved. This study has documented the fact that many of the items which are now considered essential to medical practice were not available a quarter-century ago.

CHAPTER 1
SIGNIFICANT MEDICAL ADVANCES
LISTED BY MEDICAL SPECIALTIES

The purpose of the survey on scientific medical advances was to obtain a list of developments which occurred during the quarter century 1936 to 1962, that are considered important in the practice of medicine. The inquiry was limited to clinical medicine and to developments that were actually in use and not in the research stage. It was intended that a rather concise list or summary of important scientific advances used in clinical medicine be presented in a fashion that would be meaningful.

To accomplish this goal, several alternative methods were considered. It was finally decided to survey numerous qualified physicians within the specialty areas of medicine and general practice and to ask questions pertinent only to their own areas of practice. The questionnaires asked for the significant advances within the various specialties and general practice. The physicians surveyed were not asked to list advances in all areas of medicine.

A major problem was to determine the criterion to use in judging a significant advance in order that physicians in the various specialties and in general practice would make their decisions on a uniform basis. Several possible criteria were suggested: a significant advance is one that has been life-saving; cost-reducing; time-reducing; etc. After much consideration the following criterion was established: "A significant advance is one which medical practitioners would least like to do without in their own practice of medicine." One advantage of this criterion is that not every specialty can claim life-saving advances and certainly not all advances are cost-reducing. This criterion allows for flexibility, i.e., it permits the individual physician to establish his own criterion in judging those advances he would least like to do without in his practice of medicine.

A list of advances in a certain specialty was sent to the physicians being surveyed in that specialty. The lists were intended to serve as catalysts or stimulants to the physician indicating the type of information desired. The physician was free to ignore all the items on the list and write in his own ideas if he wished.

Twenty-three areas of medicine were covered in the survey.
Anesthesiology
Dermatology
Diseases of the Chest
Experimental Medicine and Therapeutics
Gastroenterology and Proctology
General Practice
Internal Medicine
Neurological Surgery
Nuclear Medicine
Obstetrics and Gynecology
Ophthalmology
Orthopedic Surgery
Otolaryngology
Pathology
Pediatrics
Physical Medicine and Rehabilitation
Plastic Surgery
Preventive Medicine
Psychiatry and Neurology
Radiology
Surgery
Thoracic Surgery
Urology

CHOOSING A SAMPLE OF PHYSICIANS
Twenty physicians from each of the 22 specialties and from general practice were chosen, with the exception of Experimental Medicine and Therapeutics (fourteen physicians only). No attempt was made to weight the specialty groups in accordance with the per cent of the total physician population they represent.

Names of qualified specialists in each of the areas to be surveyed were chosen from the following organizations:

1. The Advisory Board for Medical Specialties (19 medical specialties represented).
2. The A.M.A. Scientific Sections (19 medical specialties represented).
3. The A.M.A. Residency Review Committees (16 medical specialties represented).
4. Editors of some of the specialty journals and medical yearbooks and officers of some of the specialty associations.

When a specialty was represented by each of the groups listed, as equal a number of physicians as possible was chosen from each organization. However, not every specialty surveyed was represented in all organizations. In these cases as equal a number of specialists as possible was chosen from the remaining groups. A reserve of names was kept for use in cases where replacements were needed.

A list of advances in one of the specialty areas or general practice, a covering letter and an instruction sheet were sent to each of the 454 physicians initially contacted.

A preliminary review of the responses indicated that in a majority of the specialties two-thirds to three-fourths of the physicians surveyed had responded. Six specialties, however, had considerably less than a two-thirds response. In order to obtain a better response, physicians who had not responded were eliminated and survey material was sent to other physicians. By resampling in these six groups, at least a two-thirds response was achieved in all the specialties surveyed. The total response over the entire sample was slightly over 75 per cent.

Instruction sheets were mailed to the panel, requesting that the following procedures be followed:

1. Medical advances were to be chosen from scientific developments of the last twenty-five years, i.e., from 1936 to 1962.
2. A significant advance is a development which the physician could least do without in his area of specialization.
3. Each physician was to limit his selection to ten advances.
4. All advances could be selected from the lists provided, all could be written in by the physician, or they could be arrived at through a combination of both methods.

A slightly different request was made in the letters and instruction sheets sent to physicians in the areas of Experimental Medicine and Therapeutics, Plastic Surgery and Nuclear Medicine. Since preliminary lists of advances were not prepared in these specialties, it was necessary to ask that physicians list ten or fewer developments in their own field.

TABULATION OF THE RESPONSES

Upon receipt of a physician's response, a record was made of the advances chosen by him. Master lists for 20 of the specialties were maintained. At the conclusion of the survey period, January 31, 1963, the votes each coded item received were totalled. All advances written in by the physicians were added to the appropriate master lists.

Advances chosen within each of the 22 lists were subsequently ranked in order of frequency, with the advance receiving the greatest percentage of the votes on the top and so on down the list. Whenever two or more developments received the same percentage, the items were listed alphabetically. All ad-

vances receiving less than 15% of the votes were excluded from the list.

Table 1 presents the percentage distribution of responses received from each specialty. A low response was received from physicians in Experimental Medicine and Therapeutics. Responses from that specialty have been excluded from the final tabulations.

TABLE I
DISTRIBUTION OF RESPONSES BY SPECIALTY

SPECIALTY	NUMBER RESPONDING	PER CENT RESPONDING
Anesthesiology	20	100
Dermatology	16	80
Diseases of the Chest	16	80
Experimental Medicine and Therapeutics	6	43
Gastroenterology and Proctology	14	70
General Practice	17	85
Internal Medicine	18	90
Neurological Surgery	16	80
Nuclear Medicine	14	65
Obstetrics and Gynecology	18	90
Ophthalmology	15	75
Orthopedic Surgery	19	95
Otolaryngology	19	95
Pathology	17	85
Pediatrics	15	75
Physical Medicine and Rehabilitation	14	70
Plastic Surgery	17	85
Preventive Medicine, Public Health, Occupational Medicine, Aerospace Medicine	16	80
Psychiatry and Neurology	17	85
Radiology	15	75
Surgery	17	85
Thoracic Surgery	16	70
Urology	19	95

RESULTS OF THE SURVEY

As a result of this survey, the Commission prepared 22 separate lists of medical advances. Because of the design of the survey, the Commission did not attempt to make an over-all analysis or single list. The study has provided the profession and the public with a multiple listing of what physicians in the early 1960's think are the most significant medical advances of the past quarter century. The listing follows.

SIGNIFICANT ADVANCES AND TECHNOLOGICAL DEVELOPMENTS

Anesthesiology

Muscle relaxants
    Succinylcholine
    Tubocurarine
    Gallamine

Recognition of value and standard use of recovery room

General anesthetic agents
  Fluothane (Halothane)
  Cyclopropane
  Trichlorethylene
Improved methods of cardiac resuscitation
Development of modern ventilators, assistors and improved methods for artificial respiration, e.g., Ambu respirator
Development and increasing use of operating room monitors (flowmeter, electro-cardiogram, cardiac monitor)
Development of hypothermia
Refinements in soda lime CO_2 absorption
Local anesthetic agents
  Lidocaine
  Mepiracaine
Standardization of anesthetic equipment
Better equipment for pediatric anesthesia, e.g., Digby-leigh valve and other unidirectional valves, improved endotracheal equipment
Pin index safety system for gas cylinders

Dermatology
Corticosteroids and ACTH
  (topical, systemic and intralesional use)
Antibotics for use against bacteria (systemic), e.g.,
  Penicillins
  Tetracyclines
  Erythromycin
  Streptomycin
Antibiotics for use against fungi (systemic), e.g.,
  Griseofulvin
  Nystatin
  Amphotericin B
Increased recognition of systemic diseases and syndromes manifested in the skin
Development of Treponema pallidum immobilization test
Antihistamines
Sulfa drugs, e.g.,
  Sulfadimethoxine
  Sulfapyridine
  Sulfisoxazole
Antimalarials
Antimetabolites
Use of ultraviolet light in diagnosis of fungal infections
Sulfones—for leprosy and dermatitis herpetiformis
Advances in delineation of etiologies of contact dermatitis (e.g., cosmetics)

Diseases of the Chest
Antibiotics, in particular,
  Penicillins
Antituberculosis chemotherapy
  Isoniazid
  Para-aminosalicylic acid (PAS)
  Streptomycin
Improvements in bronchoscopy
Development of exfoliative cytology
Improvements in planigraphy
Angiocardiography (angiography) including angiopneumography
Development and improvement of various intracutaneous tests (histoplasmin, tuberculin)
Improvements in bronchography
Isoproterenol
Techniques for evaluation of pulmonary function
Anatomy of the lungs—recognition of importance of bronchopulmonary segment—made possible definite surgical and medical therapy
Inhalational therapy including ventilatory aids such as IPPB (intermittent positive pressure breathing)
Major exploratory, resective, extirpative pulmonary surgery
Corticosteroids

Gastroenterology and Proctology
Antibiotics, e.g.,
  Chloramphenicol
  Drugs for intestinal tract sterilization
  Neomycin
  Tetracyclines
Cholangiography and cholecystography
Needle liver biopsy
ACTH and corticosteroids
Cytodiagnosis in gastric carcinoma
Liver function tests (e.g., BSP)
Mucosal biopsy capsules
Improved esophagoscopes
Amebicides (e.g., chloroquine)
Esophageal tamponade balloon
Improved gastroscopes
Use of radioisotopes
  Chromium 51 tagged red blood cells
  In metabolic studies (e.g., fat uptake)

General Practice
Antibiotics, e.g.,
  Penicillins
  Tetracyclines

Acceptance of widespread immunization programs
  Poliomyelitis vaccines
  Measles vaccines
  Influenza vaccines
  Tetanus toxoid
Oral hypoglycemic agents
More widespread psychiatric counseling and understanding of the mentally ill
Tranquilizers
More frequent physical examinations
Introduction of oral contraceptives
Corticosteroids
Effective oral diuretics
Modified insulin
Psychomotor stimulants
Sulfonamides
Antihypertensive drugs
Increased community-doctor interest in poison control

Internal Medicine

Antibiotics, e.g.,
  Penicillins
  Tetracyclines
  Chloramphenicol
Cardiac catheterization
Serum electrolyte determinations
Use of corticosteroids
  Collagen diseases
  Dermatological disorders
  Allergic diseases
  Renal diseases
  True nephrotic syndrome
  Ulcerative colitis
Use of radioisotopes in diagnosis and treatment
  I^{131} in thyroid abnormalities
  Blood volume studies
  Fat absorption studies
  B-12 absorption studies with iron and chromium
  Localization of brain tumors
  Treatment of malignant diseases
  Polycythemia
  Treatment of pituitary tumors
Antihypertensive agents
Antituberculosis chemotherapy
  Isoniazid
  Para-aminosalicylic acid (PAS)
  Streptomycin
Artificial kidney
Effective oral diuretics

Introduction of and improvements in hormonal therapy of
  Lymphomas
  Leukemias
  Breast cancer
  Prostate cancer
Recognition of nutritional abnormalities as etiologies of disease
  Vitamin deficiency
  Essential amino acid deficiency
  Relation of diet to hepatic pathology
Serum and urinary hormone levels in relation to endocrine disorders
Introduction of and improvements in hormone replacement therapy of
  Diabetes
  Hypothyroidism
  Hypoadrenalism
Antimalarial drugs
Oral hypoglycemic agents
Tranquilizers
Collection and handling of blood and blood products
External cardiac massage
Liver function tests (e.g., BSP)
Refinements in anticoagulants

Neurological Surgery

Development of cerebral angiography
Development of stereotactic surgery with its advances in electrophysiology and the various methods of producing lesions of controlled size (ultrasound, chemical, electrocoagulation, cyrosurgery)
Surgical treatment of vascular lesions of brain (e.g., aneurysms) and angiomatous malformations
Development of drains in hydrocephalus
Development of fractional pneumoencephalography
Development of myelography
Use of radioisotopes in the diagnosis and localization of intracranial lesions
Use of hypothermia in neurosurgical procedures
Control of increased intracranial pressure (intravenous urea, hypotension, positive-negative respiration)
Cranioplasty with alloplastic materials (tantulum, plastics, stainless steel and other alloplastic materials)
Anticonvulsants
Corticosteroids
Perfection of prefrontal and fractional lobotomy
Perfection of spinothalamic tractotomy

Antibiotics

The diagnosis and treatment of protruded cervical discs including myelography, discography and anterior fusion.

Perfection of rhizotomy

Tracheostomy for extensive brain surgery

Nuclear Medicine

Radioisotopes for diagnostic purposes, in particular,
  For detection and diagnosis of thyroid disease
  For determination of plasma and blood volume and in the determination of blood circulation
  For study of kidney function and for detection and diagnosis of certain kidney diseases
  For study of protein metabolism
  For detection and diagnosis of brain tumors
  For detection and diagnosis of pancreatic insufficiency

Scanning with radioisotopes and the development of scanning equipment
  Scintillation scanning

Treatment of the thyroid with radioiodine
  Hyperthyroidism
  Thyroid malignancies

Use of radiophosphorus (for diagnostic and therapeutic purposes), in particular,
  Treatment of polycythemia
  Blood volume determination
  Treatment of chronic leukemia
  Treatment of certain lymphomas

Utilization of radioisotopes for diagnosis (exclusive of those mentioned specifically on the list)

The advent of practical telecobalt therapy for general cancer treatment (Cobalt bomb)

Radioactive cobalt tagged vitamin employed in a specific diagnostic test for pernicious anemia

Radioactive iron
  For measurement of the total circulating red cell mass
  For the study of red cell life and production
  For the study of blood diseases

Radioactive chromium
  For blood volume studies
  For bone marrow function studies
  For study of red cell life
  For study of blood diseases

Utilization of radioactive isotopes for therapy (exclusive of those mentioned specifically in the list)

Obstetrics and Gynecology

Papanicolaou test for cytodiagnosis of cervical cancer

Penicillins

Increasing knowledge of Rh and ABO incompatabilities

Recognition of fibrinogen deficiency

Development of chemotherapy of choriocarcinoma

Radiation treatment in cancer of female pelvic organs

Increasing number of routine examinations of breast and pelvic organs

Pitocin

Improvement in prenatal care leading to decreased incidence of toxemia in pregnancy

Improvement in treatment of diabetes in pregnancy

Improvements in methods of child spacing
  Oral contraceptives
  Improvements in mechanical contraceptives

Improvement in radical hysterectomy and node dissection

Recognition of rubella in the 1st trimester as a cause of congenital malformations

Adrenal corticosteroids

Development of electrocardiography of the fetus prior to and during delivery

Increasing knowledge of the etiologies of sterility

Progestational hormones

Ophthalmology

Discovery of the role of excessive oxygen as a cause of retrolental fibroplasia when administered to premature infants

Use of antibiotics and sulfonamides in the treatment of many infections of the eye (use of sulfonamide in trachoma)

Use of carbonic anhydrase inhibitors, such as acetazolamide, in the treatment of glaucoma

Corticosteroids for inflammatory conditions of the eye

Improvements in gonioscopy

Improved methods of treating detached retina, including scleral buckling with encircling plastic band and photocoagulation

Recognition of toxoplasmosis as a cause of uveitis

Perfection of methods for successfully using corneal transplants

Improvements in tonometry

Improvement in contact lenses and their use for wide variety of visual problems

Advances in the treatment of retinoblastoma

The identification of the trachoma virus with potential for developing a successful vaccine

The discovery of idoxuridine in the treatment of herpes simplex keratitis

Alpha-chymotrypsin in cataract surgery

Electroretinography

Goldmann applanation tonometry

Use of antibiotics in the treatment of gonorrhea and syphilis preventing ophthalmic complications from these two venereal infections

Orthopedic Surgery

Antibiotics, e.g.,
    Penicillins
    Streptomycin
    Tetracyclines
    Chloramphenicol

Antituberculosis chemotherapy
    Isoniazid (INH)
    Para-aminosalicylic acid (PAS)
    Streptomycin

Corticosteroids

Plastic and metal implants

Improved artificial limbs

Radiology
    Arteriography
    Radio-opaque myelography with the use of iophendylate and other safe contrast media for radiological diagnosis

Advances in surgery of trauma, e.g., skin grafting, internal fixation of fractures

Advances in reconstructive and restorative surgery, especially surgical care of arthritic joints, hands, elbows, knees and feet

Functional extremity splints

The Kuntscher and other types of intra medullary nails for fractures of long bones

Medullary prostheses to replace head and neck of femur following trauma and arthritis

Advances in manipulative treatment (i.e., cervical or lumbar traction)

Advances in surgery of the hand

Use of preserved bones (bone banks)

Acid and alkaline phosphotase levels with associated connotations

Advances in fracture reduction

Poliomyelitis vaccines

Radioisotopes for diagnostic and therapeutic use

Otolaryngology

Stapes surgery

Antibiotics, e.g.,

    Penicillins
    Tetracyclines
    Chloramphenicol
    Streptomycin

Surgical microscope

Audiometry (and associated developments and improvements in audiometers, in particular, the Bekesy audiometer)

Development of programs emphasizing early auditory and speech training in children with impaired hearing

Myringoplasty and tympanoplasty

Improvements in and miniaturization of hearing aids

Miniaturized surgical instruments

Fenestration surgery

Antihistamines

Correction of Meniere's disease

Surgical treatment of malignancies of larynx and pharynx

Reconstructive nasal surgery

Advances in prevention of hearing loss
    Industrial use of ear plugs
    Conservation of hearing programs in industry

Corticosteroids

Pathology

Development of blood banks with subsequent improvements in collection, processing, storage and administration of blood and its derivatives

Exfoliative cytology in diagnosis of cervical cancer

Isolation and identification of many viruses

Enzyme determination (e.g., SGOT, amylase, alkaline and acid phosphatase)

Fluorescent antibody technique

Electrolyte determination

Hormone determination

Improvements in microscopy (e.g., phase contrast, electron)

Chromosome counts and mapping (e.g., in mongolism, Kleinfelter's Syndrome)

Quantitative and qualitative colormetric procedures
    Liver function tests
    Kidney function tests

Automation in the laboratory

Improvements in cell, tissue and organ culture for basic investigations in cell biology and for practical clinical research in microbiology, biochemistry and chemotherapy

Use of radiosotopes in studying thyroid function,

measuring blood volume, determining life span of erythrocyte, pancreatic function, etc.

Pediatrics

Penicillin and the broad spectrum antibiotics
Development of exchange transfusions in erythroblastosis fetalis
Development of vaccines and improvements in immunization programs
  Poliomyelitis vaccines
  Measles vaccine
  Tetanus, pertussis, diphtheria vaccines
Delineation of inborn errors of metabolism
Recognition of etiology of retrolental fibroplasia
Recognition of chromosomal abnormalities in certain genetic diseases (e.g., mongolism)
Recognition of maternal infections as bases for congenital malformations (e.g., rubella) and infections (e.g., toxoplasmosis)
Clinical management of fluid and electrolyte imbalance, especially for severe diarrheas and diabetic coma
Corticosteroids
Diagnosis and management of congenital heart defects by cardiac catheterization, angiocardiography, and surgical correction
Isoniazid, streptomycin, para-aminosalicylic acid
  Treatment of tuberculosis and also its role in the prevention of complications such as meningitis
Delineation of patterns of normal growth and development (child development, child psychiatry)
Discovery and identification of many viruses—respiratory, myxoviruses, ECHO, adenovirus, etc.

Physical Medicine and Rehabilitation

Electromyography, nerve conduction velocity determination and other electrodiagnostic techniques
Improvements in prosthetic devices
Refined techniques and equipment for therapeutic exercise
  Cervical and lumbar traction
  Progressive resistive exercises
  Proprioceptive facilitation techniques
  Neuromuscular re-education
Advances in medical rehabilitation
  Development of the concept of total medical rehabilitation care
  Widespread establishment of rehabilitation centers
  Development of pre-vocational evaluation techniques

Development of rehabilitation nursing
Technical advances in speech therapy
Development of comprehensive programs for rehabilitation of severely disabled
Antibiotics, e.g.,
  Penicillin
  Tetracyclines
  Chloramphenicol
Development of functional orthetic devices and splints
Psychomotor stimulants
Surgical plastic and metal implants
Tranquilizers
Gait training
Newer sulfa drugs
Shortwave, microwave and ultrasonic diathermy

Plastic Surgery

Improved treatment of burns
  Better knowledge of electrolytes and fluid requirements in treatment of burns
  Early coverage of burn wounds with skin grafts to minimize residual scar deformity and contracture
  Application of early debridement of the deeply burned surface in order to forestall late septic complications
Dermatomes (Reese, Padgett, Barker and Brown)
Improved anesthetic agents and techniques
  General anesthetics and techniques
  Local anesthetics and techniques
  Block and inhalation anesthetic agents
  Development of endotracheal anesthesia which has permitted rapid progress in head and neck surgery
  Development of hypothermic procedures
Developments in cleft lip and cleft palate repair
Advances in the transplantation and homotransplantation of tissues along with a better understanding of host immune reaction
Improvements in the use of blood and blood components
  Blood banking and greater availability of blood
  Development of blood substitutes
  Refined transfusion techniques
  Development of methods for preparation of plasma free from viral hepatitis
Development of inert synthetic materials for use in reconstructive surgery
  Implantation at surface depths
  Sub-cutaneous implantation to restore form and contour

172

Advances in hand surgery

Antibiotics and antibacterials

Advances in repair of maxillofacial injuries

Ready availability of very fine atraumatic suture materials

Improvement in the areas of dressing materials, tapes and cleansing agents

Improved understanding of wound management

Preventive Medicine

Development and more general uses of vaccines, e.g.,
Influenza
Poliomyelitis
Smallpox (newer types)
Tetanus, pertussis, diphtheria (newer types)
Yellow fever

Increased emphasis on health of employees, e.g.,
Improvements in the care of the handicapped and injured worker
Physical examinations in industry
Pre-employment examinations and matching of jobs to capabilities
Progress in the understanding of sickness absence
Study and treatment of alcoholism

Increased community-doctor interest:
In accidents
In athletic injury control
In health maintenance programs, especially among the aging
In poison control
In pre- and post-natal care

Providing a safe and healthful workplace in industry and commerce in the face of increased manufacture and the use of hazardous physical and chemical agents, e.g.,
Introduction of and compulsory use of protective equipment
Safety education programs

More frequent physical examinations (principle of voluntary periodic examinations as a means of early detection of disease)

Development of insecticides (e.g., DDT)

Fluoridation of public drinking water

Mass diagnostic surveys, e.g.,
Blood pressure tests on a mass screening basis
Detection of diabetes mellitus
Papanicolaou smears for cytodiagnosis of cancer
X-ray for tuberculosis and other chest lesions

Developments in the telemetering of physiological data and the application of this knowledge to aerospace travel

Diet
Better awareness of dietary needs by the American people
Knowledge of the need for vitamins

Improved status and development of mental hygiene programs (assistance of psychopharmacology)

Improvements in industrial hygiene engineering, e.g.,
Lighting
Ventilation

Antimalarial drugs

The community and public health
A better informed public in relation to personal and community health
Community health centers
Modern departments of health at state and local levels
Sanitation procedures and laws
Use of the public health unit in rural areas

Delineation of etiologies of contact dermatitis

Recognition and delineation of pneumoconiosis

Studies in stress reaction (isolation, cold, heat, noise, fatigue, anoxia, etc.)

Psychiatry and Neurology

Developments in electroencephalography

Changing attitudes toward mental disease, as illustrated by
Teaching of emotional problems in medical schools
Use of the halfway house
Open door policies of large mental hospitals
Psychiatric units in general hospitals and other developments

Anticonvulsants

Cerebral angiography

Tranquilizers

Development of electro shock treatment

Psychomotor stimulants

Improvements in myelography

Advances in psychotherapy

Chemotherapy for central nervous system syphilis and bacterial meningitis, e.g.,
Penicillin and other antibiotics

Fractional pneumoencephalogram

Advances in neuro-physiology, neuro-psychopharmacology and neuro-biochemistry

Antiparkinson agents

Development of child psychiatry

Development of electromyography

Metabolic and genetic information about mental deficiency and certain diseases of the nervous system

Radiology

Angiocardiography, angiography (arteriography)
  Development of new concentrated vascular radiopaque media of low toxicity
  Development of rapid film sequencing equipment, automatic injectors and arterial catheters for cardiovascular roentgenology
Improvements and developments in fluoroscopy
  Image intensifier
  Cine-radiography
  Use of television circuits in fluoroscopy
Improvements in radiation therapy and therapy equipment
  Supervoltage therapy
  Teletherapy units (Co-60 and Ce)
  Rotational therapy
  Refinements in dosimetry
  Oxygen as a radiosensitizer
  BUDR sensitization of DNA
I^{131} in diagnosis and treatment of thyroid abnormalities
Improvements in planigraphy
Automatic x-ray film processing and exposure control
Improvements in intravenous pyelography
Improvements in myelography
Use of radioactive substance in diagnosis and treatment of brain tumors
Chromium tagged red blood cells
Fractional pneumoencephalography
Improvements in operative and intravenous cholangiography and cholecystography

Surgery

Improved pre- and post-operative care
  Blood banks
  Controlled or assisted respiration
  Early ambulation
  Fluid and electrolytes
  Heparin and dicumarol
  Plasma, serum albumin and fibrinogen
  Vitamin K
Antibiotics and antimicrobials
  Penicillins
  Chloramphenicol
  Neomycin
  Tetracyclines
Vascular surgery
Cholangiography and cholecystography
Vascular prostheses and homografts
Arteriography

Vagotomy
Cardiac surgery (including open heart surgical procedures employing extracorporeal circulation and hypothermia)
Establishment of tissue banks (blood vessels, bones, skin, etc.)
Cancer chemotherapeutic agents, e.g.,
  Mechlorethamine HCL
Organ transplantation
Isolation and perfusion of tumors

Thoracic Surgery

Antibiotics, e.g.,
  Penicillins
  Streptomycin
  Tetracyclines
  Chloramphenicol
Use of extracorporeal circulation
Access to cardiac chambers, e.g., mitral commissurotomy
Refinements in pneumonectomy (recognition of the bronchopulmonary unit as a surgical unit)
Antituberculosis chemotherapy
  Para-aminosalicylic acid (PAS)
  Isoniazid (INH)
  Streptomycin
Hypothermia
Arteriography
Cardiac catheterization
Surgical correction of aortic aneurysms
Cardiac resuscitation
Closure of patent ductus
Improvements in bronchoscopy
Resection of coarctation
Valvular and arterial prostheses
Controlled cardiac arrest during surgery
Improvements in bronchogram
Improvements in respirators

Urology

Improvements in intravenous pyelography, angiography and cineradiography
Discovery of the relationship of prostatic carcinoma, and certain other neoplasms, to hormone balance with the development of orchiectomy, androgen and estrogen therapy as control measures
Development of safe, effective antimicrobial, antifungal, and antituberculosis agents for control of virtually every significant pathogenic organism encountered in the genito-urinary tract

Advances in prostatic surgery by both open and endoscopic use

Advances in urinary diversion procedures and the use of intestinal segments as substitutes for ureters, bladder or urethra

Advances in renal vascular surgery, renal transplantation in identical twins, and progress toward success in other transplantations

Development of techniques for hemodialysis and peritoneal dialysis

Development of improved agencies in the control of carcinoma, including electrocautery, chemotherapy, radiation and radioactive isotopes in addition to radical surgical techniques

Improved identification, understanding and rehabilitation of intersex problems

New and improved optical, electrical and mechanical instruments for diagnostic and therapeutic use

CHAPTER 2
SIGNIFICANT PHARMACEUTICAL ADVANCES

A search of the literature on medical advances indicated that many breakthroughs were possible, in part, because of certain drug developments. Moreover, physicians participating in the preceding survey frequently listed drugs among their choices of significant developments. Although the lists in Chapter 1 include a great number of pharmaceuticals, they do not provide a complete review of drug developments during the past twenty-five years.

The need for a systematic review of developments in the pharmaceutical industry was obvious. The Pharmaceutical Manufacturers Association, representing manufacturers of prescription products, supplied a list of new single chemical entity drugs introduced to the United States market between 194 and 1962. The American Medical Association's De partment of Drugs compiled a similar list of produc introduced during the period 1935-1941, and assiste in the development of a survey to determine th most significant therapeutic agents or groups drugs developed since 1934. The results of this su vey are presented in Table 1. The thirty pharmace ticals mentioned most frequently in survey response are listed in descending order of "votes" receive from 304 consultants. The table also includes bri descriptions of therapeutic uses of these drugs. Mo detailed tabulations of the survey results are pr sented in Table 4.

TABLE 1
THIRTY IMPORTANT THERAPEUTIC AGENTS NOW IN USE IN THE UNITED STATES AND INTRODUCED SINCE 1934

10 basic Penicillins, plus salts and esters
Antibacterial drugs which are used primarily in the treatment of infections of the skin, respiratory tract, and the genito-urinary tract.

Adrenocorticosteroids
More than 20 synthetic adrenal hormones and their chemical derivatives. They are used primarily in the treatment of "collagen diseases" (e.g., rheumatoid arthritis and various forms of allergy).

Vaccines (poliomyelitis, measles, influenza, etc.)
For the prevention or modification of infectious diseases like poliomyelitis, measles, influenza, etc.

Synthetic anticoagulants
Used to prevent formation or extension of blood clots within arteries and veins (e.g., coronary thrombosis, thrombophlebitis).

Streptomycin
An important antibiotic, one of the primary drugs for treating tuberculosis.

Isoniazid
The most important drug in the treatment and prophylaxis of tuberculosis.

Chlorpromazine and other tranquilizers
Over 30 compounds with mild depressant action on the brain, used in certain mental illnesses and anxiety states, and for antinauseant and sedative effects.

Hydantoins
Used in the treatment of grand mal epilepsy, and certain other convulsive states.

Diphenhydramine and 30 other antihistaminics
Employed mainly in treating certain allergic conditic and also for antiemetic and sedative effects.

Thiazides
To remove excess fluid from the body in certain type of heart and kidney diseases. Also used in the treatmer of hypertension (high blood pressure).

Sulfonamides
Used in the treatment of infections of the respirator and urinary tracts, and in certain types of meningiti

Tetracycline derivatives, plus salts and esters
Used in the treatment of a wide variety of disease caused by many different types of microorganisms.

Rauwolfia and Veratrum alkaloids
Principles of plant origin used in treating hypertension or as a sedative or tranquilizer.

Meperidine
A powerful pain relieving drug.

Chloramphenicol
An important broad-spectrum antibiotic which is use in the treatment of typhoid fever, certain types of foo poisoning, and in other infections caused by microor ganisms which are resistant to other antibiotics.

Oral antidiabetes agents
Replacement for insulin in some types of diabetes.

Chloroquin compounds
Antimalarial and antiamebic drugs also used in a few unrelated diseases as arthritis.

(Table 1 continued)

176

TABLE 1 (cont.)

Antithyroid agents
A group of unrelated compounds ranging from propylthiouracil to radio-iodide, for treating hyperthyroidism.

Immune globulins
A protein derived from human blood which, when injected into persons exposed to certain infectious diseases, confers temporary immunity to the disease.

Aminosalicylic acid, salts and esters
Important drugs which are used in the treatment of tuberculosis.

Isoproterenol
Used in the treatment of bronchial asthma to relieve the spasm of the bronchial tubes.

Methantheline and other anticholinergics
Parasympatholytic agents used in cases of peptic ulcer and to decrease hypermotility or spasm of the gastrointestinal tract.

Ganglionic blocking agents, mostly quaternary ammonium compounds
Used in the treatment of certain types of hypertension (high blood pressure).

Phenylephrine
A drug which is used to shrink swollen nasal mucous membranes and to clear nasal passages.

Halogenated hydrocarbon anesthetics
Volatile liquids which are used for inhalation anesthesia.

Surgical skeletal muscle relaxants about 7 surgical, peripherally acting preparations
These drugs are used as muscle relaxants during surgical operations.

Organomercurial diuretics
To remove excess fluid from the body in certain diseases of the heart, liver, and kidneys.

Estrogen-progestogen contraceptives
Oral contraceptive agents.

Trihexyphenidyl and other antiparkinsonism agents
To relieve the muscle stiffness and tremor in patients with Parkinson's disease.

Hypnotic barbiturates
Sedatives and sleeping pills.

Lidocaine and other local anesthetics
Injected locally to anesthetize the tissues prior to minor surgical operations.

THE QUESTIONNAIRE

On August 2, 1963, a questionnaire listing 89 drugs or groups of drugs was mailed to 380 medical specialists. Each consultant was asked to indicate the thirty items which he considers the most significant developments during the survey period. Additional space was provided to write in names of drugs which did not appear on the questionnaire. The explanatory letter and the questionnaire are included with this chapter as Exhibits 1 and 2.

A *Significant Advance* was defined as one which has greatly benefited mankind and the medical profession. An alternative definition would be "a single chemical entity or group of drugs, which physicians could least do without." Preference for a definition depended upon the physicians' judgment of what constitutes progress. The panel was asked to consider only therapeutic agents introduced in the U.S. during 1935-1962. They were asked *not* to use prescription volume or other economic bases in making a selection.

The following procedure was used to select the 89 drugs listed in the questionnaire:

(a) The Commission staff reduced the number of all drugs developed during 1935-1962 to 140, using prescription volumes reported in National Disease and Therapeutic Index surveys.

(b) The AMA Department of Drugs constructed a separate list of 120 therapeutic agents

which they considered important.

(c) The 89 drugs appearing on the questionnaire were finally chosen from the two lists.

In several instances it was necessary to list classes of drugs rather than specific drugs, in order to present a short list. For example, in considering the 30-odd antihistaminics, it was decided to indicate the drug first introduced in the U.S. market with the words "and 30 others." By selecting this item, a consultant selected all antihistaminics.

Pharmaceuticals were listed according to the latest United States Pharmacopoeia classification (U.S.P. XVII) which will become official in 1965.

THE PANEL

A sample of 397 physicians and pharmacologists was selected from the list of 2,780 consultants to the AMA Council on Drugs. An alphabetical card file is maintained by the Department of Drugs, with complete information on the educational background and professional qualifications of each consultant. Systematically, one out of every seven cards was chosen, and the consultant's biographical information evaluated.

Table 2 presents the distribution of consultants by specialty and the distribution of the sample selected. Seventeen of the 397 consultants were eliminated *either* because they had died or their current address was not available, or they had indicated that they did not wish to receive survey materials.

TABLE 2
SPECIALTY DISTRIBUTION OF CONSULTANTS TO THE AMA COUNCIL ON DRUGS, AND OF THE SELECTED SAMPLE

SPECIALTIES	TOTAL CONSULTANTS	NUMBER IN SAMPLE
Anesthesiology	113	20
Biochemistry	12	—
Dentistry	1	—
Dermatology	121	17
Internal Medicine	363	31
Allergy	23	3
Arthritis and Rheumatology	44	8
Cardiovascular Diseases	150	26
Endocrinology	70	6
Gastroenterology	92	19
Hematology	97	8
Infectious Diseases	49	10
Metabolic Disorders	51	9
Pediatrics	107	40
Pulmonary Diseases	48	7
Microbiology	63	7
Neurology and Psychiatry	329	51
Obstetrics and Gynecology	162	19
Ophthalmology	91	10
Otolaryngology	14	2
Parasitology	8	2
Pathology	13	1
Pharmacology	285	34
Physiology	10	3
Radiology	195	32
Surgery	175	19
Neurological Surgery	5	1
Orthopedic Surgery	26	5
Urology	63	7
TOTAL	2780	397

TABLE 3
SPECIALTY DISTRIBUTION OF SURVEY MAILING TOTAL RESPONSE, AND USABLE RESPONSE

SPECIALTIES	TOTAL MAILING	TOTAL RESPONSE	USABLE RESPONS
Anesthesiology	15	11	11
Biochemistry	4	4	4
Dentistry	—	—	—
Dermatology	17	16	15
Internal Medicine	7	5	5
Allergy	8	8	8
Arthritis and Rheumatology	9	7	7
Cardiovascular Diseases	35	32	31
Endocrinology	8	7	7
Gastroenterology	18	15	14
Hematology	13	11	11
Infectious Diseases	16	13	13
Metabolic Disorders	16	16	13
Pediatrics	10	10	9
Pulmonary Diseases	9	7	7
Microbiology	9	6	6
Neurology and Psychiatry	54	46	41
Obstetrics and Gynecology	17	15	14
Ophthalmology	10	8	8
Otolaryngology	2	1	1
Parasitology	2	2	2
Pathology	—	—	—
Pharmacology	33	24	23
Physiology	3	2	2
Radiology	30	24	22
Surgery	18	17	17
Neurological Surgery	1	0	0
Orthopedic Surgery	5	3	3
Urology	11	10	10
TOTAL	380	320 or 84%	304 or 80%

Table 3, column 1, shows the specialty distribution of the 380 persons who received questionnaires. The initial examination of the panel's background and experience disclosed that many physicians classified under "internal medicine" and "pediatrics" were qualified in the various subspecialties of these two categories. In the final listing, only the few physicians for whom detailed information was not available were classified under the broader categories of internal medicine and pediatrics. Because of this adjustment, column 2 of Table 2 differs from column 1 of Table 3.

THE RESPONSE

Approximately 320 or 84% of the questionnaire were returned. Of these, 304, or 80%, were considered usable for tabulation. Table 4 presents the per cent of consultants in each specialty who "voted" for each drug. All subspecialties of "internal medicine" were combined in column 2. Specialties with less than 20 physicians in the sample were combined under "all other" in column 7.

Many drugs in Table 4 were selected by a large percentage of the consultants in each specialty. An average of 70% of responses in each specialty mentioned the 16 drugs which received the most "votes." Variation among specialties, however, is evident in the second half of the table. For example, antiparkinsonism agents were selected by 80% of the neurologists and psychiatrists and only 9% of the radiologists. Surgical skeletal muscle relaxants were chosen by 75% of the surgeons, but by only 22% of the physicians in all subspecialties of internal medicine. The consultants' training, interests and area of experience undoubtedly caused this variation.

TABLE 4

PERCENTAGE OF RESPONDING CONSULTANTS WHO CHOSE THE THIRTY MOST OFTEN MENTIONED PHARMACEUTICALS

	TOTAL ALL SPECIALTIES	INTERNAL MEDICINE	NEUROLOGY AND PSYCHIATRY	PHARMA- COLOGY	RADIOLOGY	SURGERY	ALL OTHER
Number of Usable Returns	*304*	*125*	*41*	*23*	*22*	*20*	*73*
Penicillin	93.8	93.6	100.0	91.3	86.4	90.0	94.5
Adrenocorticosteroids	91.8	91.2	97.6	87.0	86.4	100.0	90.4
Vaccines	88.8	90.4	90.2	78.3	86.4	95.0	87.7
Synthetic Anticoagulants	87.8	89.6	82.9	87.0	81.8	95.0	87.7
Streptomycin	84.2	88.0	87.8	78.3	81.8	75.0	80.8
Isoniazid	83.9	86.4	80.5	87.0	86.4	85.0	79.5
Chlorpromazine and other Tranquilizers	83.9	83.2	97.6	87.0	68.2	90.0	79.5
Hydantoins	81.3	86.4	100.0	87.0	59.1	80.0	67.1
Diphenhydramine and 30 other Antihistaminics	80.6	77.6	90.2	82.6	81.8	80.0	79.5
Thiazides	79.6	83.2	73.2	91.3	54.5	85.0	79.5
Sulfonamides	76.6	78.4	73.2	78.3	72.7	65.0	79.5
Tetracycline Derivatives	76.6	77.6	58.5	87.0	63.6	90.0	82.2
Rauwolfia and Veratrum Alkaloids	74.3	74.4	75.6	65.2	68.2	80.0	76.7
Meperidine	71.7	73.6	65.9	69.6	59.1	75.0	75.3
Chloramphenicol	69.4	70.4	56.1	60.9	77.3	75.0	74.0
Oral Antidiabetes Agents	68.4	73.6	68.3	73.9	63.6	75.0	57.5

(Table continued)

179

TABLE 4 (cont.)

PERCENTAGE OF RESPONDING CONSULTANTS WHO CHOSE THE THIRTY MOST OFTEN MENTIONED PHARMACEUTICALS

	TOTAL ALL SPECIALTIES	INTERNAL MEDICINE	NEUROLOGY AND PSYCHIATRY	PHARMA-COLOGY	RADIOLOGY	SURGERY	ALL OTHER
Number of Usable Returns	304	125	41	23	22	20	73
Chloroquin Compounds	65.1	73.6	58.5	87.0	54.5	35.0	58.9
Antithyroid Agents	60.2	62.4	61.0	56.5	59.1	70.0	54.8
Immune Globulins	59.2	58.4	56.1	30.4	50.0	70.0	71.2
Aminosalicylic Acids	57.6	56.0	46.3	69.6	72.7	80.0	52.1
Isoproterenol	52.3	56.0	41.5	69.6	40.9	70.0	45.2
Anticholinergics	46.1	40.8	68.3	21.7	59.1	40.0	47.9
Ganglionic Blocking Agents	42.1	52.8	41.5	34.8	22.7	25.0	37.0
Phenylephrine	41.8	32.8	46.3	39.1	54.5	55.0	47.9
Halogenated Hydrocarbon Anesthetics	39.8	28.8	34.1	52.2	50.0	65.0	47.9
Surgical Skeletal Muscle Relaxants Peripherally Acting Preparations	36.8	21.6	58.5	47.8	22.7	75.0	41.1
Organomercurial Diuretics	36.5	43.2	19.5	60.9	45.5	25.0	27.4
Estrogen-Progestogen Contraceptives	35.9	32.8	46.3	34.8	31.8	35.0	37.0
Antiparkinsonism Agents	35.5	32.0	80.5	34.8	9.1	35.0	24.7
Hypnotic Barbiturates	33.9	33.6	34.1	26.1	45.5	35.0	32.9
Lidocaine and other Local Anesthetics	33.6	21.6	36.6	39.1	36.4	40.0	47.9

Appendix B to Chapter 7

DEATH RATES FOR NINE SELECTED CAUSE-OF-DEATH GROUPS, BY SEX AND AGE
UNTED STATES, 1970 AND SELECTED YEARS
(Rates per 100,000 population in specified group. Rates for earlier years adjusted for
changes in international classification of diseases)

Age Group	Tuberculosis 010-019		Poliomyelitis 040-044		Syphilis 090-097		Uterine Cancer 180-182		Rheumatic Fever with or without Heart Disease 390-398	
(In Years)	1970	1943	1970	1954	1970	1942	1970	1942	1970	1942
Male Total	3.8	48.1	0.1	1.2	0.3	4.3			6.9	22.4
Under 1	0.7	18.3	--	2.1	0.4	8.9			0.1	0.3
1-4	0.3	9.7	--	1.6	--	0.2			0.1	1.9
5-9	--	3.6	--	1.7	--	--			0.2	5.0
10-14	--	3.8	--	1.7	--	0.1			0.3	7.0
15-19	0.1	18.4	0.1	1.4	--	0.3			0.5	8.1
20-24	0.3	37.8	0.1	1.6	--	0.5			1.0	7.9
25-29	0.4	42.6	0.1	2.1	--	0.9			1.2	9.8
30-34	1.2	50.8	0.2	1.7	--	2.1			2.6	12.9
35-39	1.9	58.3	0.1	0.7	--	4.2			3.6	17.1
40-44	2.7	65.6	0.1	0.6	0.1	6.3			6.1	18.8
45-49	4.4	79.5	0.3	0.5	0.1	7.7	NOT APPLICABLE	NOT APPLICABLE	9.5	25.6
50-54	5.0	93.6	0.1	0.2	0.2	10.1			13.4	30.4
55-59	8.8	98.6	0.1	0.2	0.5	12.5			18.9	39.5
60-64	11.5	98.6	0.1	0.1	1.3	13.0			24.5	50.8
65-69	16.0	96.3	0.1	0.1	1.7	13.9			31.5	72.4
70-74	17.8	94.7	--	0.1	2.5	12.5			32.4	108.8
75-79	28.1	85.4	0.2	--	2.4	10.9			36.2	154.2
80-84	31.9	82.4	--	--	2.7	9.4			32.3	244.9
85+	36.9	68.8	--	0.3	1.3	7.4			34.7	344.4
Female Total	1.4	29.8	--	0.8	0.2	1.6	11.6	23.2	7.7	21.3
Under 1	0.2	15.6	0.1	1.8	0.2	8.5	--	--	0.1	0.4
1-4	0.3	9.5	--	1.2	--	0.2	--	--	0.1	2.0
5-9	--	3.2	--	1.5	--	--	--	--	0.1	5.9
10-14	--	6.2	--	1.2	--	0.1	--	--	0.2	7.4
15-19	0.1	26.6	--	1.1	--	0.3	0.1	0.2	0.6	8.1
20-24	0.1	45.4	--	1.3	--	0.6	0.4	1.0	0.7	8.6
25-29	0.4	44.4	0.1	1.5	--	0.8	1.6	3.5	1.3	9.5
30-34	0.7	43.6	0.1	1.2	--	1.5	3.4	10.2	2.3	13.2
35-39	1.1	37.4	0.1	0.5	--	1.7	6.1	19.9	3.6	16.6
40-44	1.4	30.5	0.1	0.3	0.2	2.3	10.4	30.8	5.6	19.1
45-49	1.7	28.4	0.1	0.3	0.1	2.6	15.8	41.5	9.0	23.5
50-54	2.1	28.4	0.1	0.2	0.2	3.0	19.9	56.6	12.3	28.5
55-59	2.4	31.1	0.1	0.2	0.2	3.6	25.0	65.6	18.2	32.5
60-64	3.1	34.4	0.1	0.1	0.5	3.6	32.4	73.7	23.9	42.0
65-69	4.3	42.5	0.1	0.1	0.6	3.5	40.7	85.0	28.6	57.5
70-74	5.6	51.2	--	--	0.8	3.3	49.2	97.8	32.3	95.1
75-79	7.1	57.4	--	--	0.8	4.1	56.3	109.0	34.9	146.4
80-84	8.8	48.9	0.1	--	1.8	3.5	57.7	116.9	33.2	223.5
85+	12.0	43.9	--	--	0.8	3.8	61.3	112.6	39.2	351.6

DEATH RATES FOR NINE SELECTED CAUSE OF DEATH GROUPS, BY SEX AND AGE:
UNITED STATES, 1970 AND SELECTED YEARS

Age Group	Hypertension and Hypertensive Heart Disease 400-404		Pneumonia 480-486		Appendicitis 540-543		Chronic Nephritis, Renal Sclerosis, and Chronic Pyelonephrites 582-584,590	
(In Years)	1970	1949	1970	1942	1970	1942	1970	1961
Male Total	10.8	29.1	33.6	46.5	0.9	6.5	7.8	11.0
Under 1	0.1	--	200.7	588.7	0.6	1.7	1.4	1.5
1-4	--	--	8.2	34.8	0.1	5.4	0.2	0.3
5-9	--	--	1.6	5.5	0.2	4.4	0.2	0.3
10-14	--	--	1.5	3.6	0.2	5.2	0.4	0.8
15-19	0.1	0.1	2.3	5.7	0.2	5.5	0.6	1.7
20-24	0.2	0.3	3.2	7.5	0.2	4.5	1.3	2.9
25-29	0.6	1.0	3.6	9.2	0.2	3.7	1.6	3.5
30-34	1.7	2.1	5.0	12.8	0.2	4.6	1.9	4.3
35-39	2.5	4.7	8.0	18.8	0.4	4.9	2.7	5.1
40-44	5.1	10.2	11.8	25.6	0.4	6.9	4.2	6.9
45-49	7.3	19.6	18.2	35.4	0.6	8.0	5.7	8.8
50-54	10.0	34.3	24.7	47.9	1.0	10.0	7.5	13.4
55-59	14.3	56.5	37.4	63.0	1.7	10.6	11.1	17.6
60-64	23.2	84.7	57.5	81.7	2.2	11.2	17.3	25.2
65-69	39.0	129.3	89.8	113.1	3.5	12.5	27.3	38.1
70-74	60.5	206.9	162.4	176.7	4.7	14.0	41.2	56.8
75-79	107.8	324.3	283.5	290.0	6.1	15.8	71.3	87.1
80-84	182.6	475.3	487.9	526.3	8.0	13.8	108.4	150.9
85+	302.2	762.8	910.8	951.8	11.1	18.5	189.2	244.5
Female Total	12.0	32.4	24.7	34.5	0.5	5.3	7.7	9.3
Under 1	0.1	--	155.3	513.5	0.3	0.3	0.8	1.3
1-4	--	--	6.4	31.8	0.2	3.4	0.1	0.2
5-9	--	--	1.7	4.7	0.1	3.2	0.2	0.4
10-14	--	--	1.3	3.6	0.2	3.9	0.3	0.8
15-19	0.1	0.1	1.7	4.4	0.1	3.0	0.6	1.5
20-24	0.1	0.4	2.2	5.5	0.1	3.1	0.9	2.0
25-29	0.4	1.0	2.7	6.8	0.1	2.6	1.3	2.8
30-34	1.1	2.5	3.3	8.4	0.2	2.7	1.8	3.5
35-39	2.3	5.6	4.9	10.7	0.2	3.6	2.7	4.3
40-44	4.2	11.1	7.1	14.9	0.2	3.9	3.8	6.0
45-49	5.6	21.0	9.3	16.6	0.3	4.7	5.0	7.6
50-54	7.7	32.6	13.2	22.7	0.3	4.6	7.3	10.9
55-59	10.3	49.7	17.5	29.1	0.8	7.7	10.7	14.1
60-64	17.4	79.4	25.7	45.9	0.8	8.2	14.3	20.4
65-69	27.6	126.4	40.5	75.7	1.2	9.0	21.9	27.5
70-74	45.8	211.0	71.5	137.3	2.0	10.1	30.5	37.3
75-79	89.4	360.6	141.5	238.2	2.7	11.2	49.2	59.1
80-84	167.2	519.6	272.6	431.2	5.5	11.3	76.0	97.6
85+	312.1	832.0	685.8	858.6	6.3	14.6	130.5	177.9

Source: Vital Statistics of the United States.

APPENDIX B TABLE 7-2

DECREASES IN RATES BETWEEN YEAR PRIOR TO DISCOVERY AND 1970, FOR SELECTED CAUSES OF DEATH
(Rates per 100,000 population in specified group. Rates for earlier years adjusted for changes in international classification of diseases)

Age Group (In Years)	1943-1970 Tuberculosis	1954-1970 Poliomyelitis	1942-1970 Syphilis	1942-1970 Uterine Cancer	1942-1970 Rheumatic Fever with or without Heart Disease	1949-1970 Hypertension and Hypertensive Heart Disease	1942-1970 Pnemonia	1942-1970 Appendicitis	1961-1970 Chronic Nephritis, Renal Scelerosis, and Chronic Pyelonephritis
Male Total	44.3	1.1	4.0		15.5	18.3	12.9	5.6	3.2
Under 1	17.6	2.1	8.5		0.2	+0.1	388.0	1.1	0.1
1-4	9.4	1.6	0.2		1.8	--	26.6	5.3	0.1
5-9	3.6	1.7	--		4.8	--	3.9	4.2	0.1
10-14	3.8	1.7	0.1	NOT APPLICABLE	6.7	--	2.0	5.0	0.4
15-19	18.3	1.3	0.3		7.6	0.0	3.4	5.3	1.1
20-24	37.5	1.5	0.5		6.9	0.1	4.3	4.3	1.6
25-29	42.2	2.0	0.9		8.6	0.4	5.6	3.5	1.9
30-34	49.6	1.5	2.1		10.3	0.4	7.8	4.4	2.4
35-39	56.4	0.6	4.2		13.5	2.2	10.8	4.5	2.4
40-44	62.9	0.5	6.2		12.7	5.1	13.8	6.5	2.7
45-49	75.1	0.2	7.6		16.1	12.3	17.2	7.4	3.1
50-54	88.6	0.1	9.9		17.0	24.3	23.2	9.0	5.9
55-59	89.8	0.1	12.0		20.6	42.2	25.6	8.0	6.5
60-64	87.1	0.0	11.7		26.3	61.5	24.2	9.0	7.9
65-69	80.3	0.0	12.2		40.9	90.3	23.3	9.0	10.8
70-74	76.9	0.1	10.0		76.4	146.4	14.3	9.3	15.6
75-79	57.3	+0.2	8.5		118.0	216.5	6.5	9.7	15.8
80-84	50.5	--	6.7		212.6	292.7	38.4	5.8	42.5
85+	31.9	0.3	6.1		309.7	460.6	41.0	7.4	55.3

	28.4	0.8	1.4	11.6	13.6	20.4	9.8	4.8	1.6
Female Total	28.4	0.8	1.4	11.6	13.6	20.4	9.8	4.8	1.6
Under 1	15.4	1.7	8.3	--	0.3	+0.1	358.2	0.0	0.5
1-4	9.2	1.2	0.2	--	1.9	--	25.4	3.2	0.1
5-9	3.2	1.5	--	--	5.8	--	3.0	3.1	0.2
10-14	6.2	1.2	0.1	--	7.2	--	2.3	3.7	0.5
15-19	26.5	1.1	0.3	0.1	7.5	0.0	2.7	2.9	0.9
20-24	45.3	1.3	0.6	0.6	7.9	0.3	3.3	3.0	1.1
25-29	40.0	1.4	0.8	1.9	8.2	0.6	4.1	2.5	1.5
30-34	42.9	1.1	1.5	6.8	10.9	1.4	5.1	2.5	1.7
35-39	36.3	0.4	1.7	13.8	13.0	3.3	5.8	3.4	1.6
40-44	29.1	0.2	2.1	20.4	13.5	6.9	7.8	3.7	2.2
45-49	26.7	0.2	2.5	25.7	14.5	15.4	7.3	4.4	2.6
50-54	26.3	0.1	2.8	36.7	16.2	24.9	9.5	4.3	3.6
55-59	28.7	0.1	3.4	40.6	14.3	39.4	11.6	6.9	3.4
60-64	31.3	0.0	3.1	41.3	18.1	62.0	21.2	7.4	6.1
65-69	38.2	0.0	2.9	44.3	28.9	98.8	35.2	7.8	5.6
70-74	45.6	--	2.5	48.6	62.8	165.2	65.8	8.1	6.8
75-79	50.3	--	3.3	52.7	111.5	271.2	96.7	8.5	9.9
80-84	40.1	+0.1	1.7	59.2	190.3	352.4	158.7	5.8	21.6
85+	31.9	--	3.0	51.3	312.4	519.9	172.8	8.3	47.4

Note: + indicates an increase; all unsigned figures represent decreases.

Source: Appendix B Table 7-1.

Part IV

INDICATORS OF THE
LEARNING OF SCIENCE

8 Indicators of Trends in the Learning of Science in High School

Edward L. Rhodes

Introduction

This chapter contains a brief analysis of indicators of the levels of performance in science by 17-year-olds and the science course enrollment trends among high school youths and relationships between the two. The study represents an attempt to focus on the trends in the amount of science learning by American youth based on data available from large-scale tests and surveys.

The education process is multidimensional. In the instance of science, the process involves both multiple inputs and multiple outputs. Examples of science inputs which can be isolated are the number of science teachers and laboratories per school or pupil and per pupil expenditures on science courses; examples of science outputs are the instilling of the scientific knowledge necessary for successful functioning in our complex society, increased economic productivity resulting from a better skilled labor force, and improved understanding of nature, within the broad range of input and output factors related to science learning. This study focuses on only one input—levels of enrollment in science courses for high school students—and on one science learning output—the possession of specific knowledge sets.

The Indicators of Science Learning: Enrollment in Science Courses

Levels of enrollment in science courses serve as measures of the education community's commitment to disbursing the knowledge of science and indicate the degree of acceptance or recognition of science as an area of study useful for adult success by both students and the community. Along these lines, the percent of the total high school student population for certain school years over a period of time enrolled in science courses has been adopted as the principal indicator of enrollment. Table 8-1 shows the percentage and absolute number of students in science courses for four time points from 1948 to 1973, in grades 7-12. For comparison, mathematics course enrollment data is also included.

To better convey the change which occurred during this "modern period" of science education, Chart 8-1, a line graph of the data in Table 8-1, is presented. As can be seen by the data from Table 8-1, the enrollment in science and mathematics courses in high school for a long period, 1948 to 1970, grew relative to the total high school enrollment, but then declined from 1970 to 1973. Although the decline was sharper for mathematics, where the percentage ratio dropped 5 points (from 76 to 71 percent), science course enrollment also declined 2 percent (from 69 to 67 percent). This 1972/73 marked decline returned the ratio of science course enrollment to total student enrollment to the levels of the early 1960s. Furthermore, the practices of curriculum design during this period (1970-73) were sufficiently stable to rule out a sudden change in course design. Therefore, the proportion of enrollments in these courses relative to total enrollments can be indicative of the percentage of students taking science courses. Between 1970/71 and 1972/73, the total student enrollment declined, which means that the percent of 12- to 17-year-old population in high school declined from 75.3 percent in 1970/71 to 72.6 percent in 1972/73. Nevertheless, the science enrollment decline with respect to total school age population was steeper, a drop from 52.3 percent in 1970/71 to 48.7 percent in 1972/73, and thus cannot be attributed to population changes. If anything, it could be argued that a higher dropout rate)possibly due to the lowering of the compulsory school age in many states) would eliminate those less likely to take science courses, and that an increase in the ratio of science course enrollment to total enrollment should be observed instead of the decline from 69.4 percent to 67.0 percent.

Table 8-2 takes a longer, historical perspective of science course enrollments, from 1890 to 1965, which encompasses 10 observation points. Included in the table are the same science and mathematics course enrollment comparisons with percentage

TABLE 8-1

ENROLLMENT IN HIGH SCHOOL SCIENCE AND MATHEMATICS COURSES IN GRADES 7-12 FOR ALL PUBLIC SCHOOLS: 1948-73

Year	Total Population (Age: 12-17)	Total Enroll. (Grades 7-12)	Enroll. Science Courses	Science % Pop.	Enroll. % Enroll.	Enroll.Math Courses	Math % Pop.	Math Enroll. % Enroll.
1948/49	12,813,140	6,907,833*	4,031,044	31.4#	58.4#	4,457,987	34.8#	64.7#
1960/61	18,970,345	11,732,742	7,739,877	40.8	66.0	8,596,396	45.3	73.3
1970/71	24,426,048	18,406,617	12,772,195	52.3	69.4	14,137,090	57.9	76.8
1972/73	24,917,753	18,104,477	12,130,000	48.7	67.0	12,855,000	51.6	71.0

*All total enrollment and course enrollment figures are expansions of a surveyed sample of the nation's schools. Thus caution should be taken when comparing these statistics to other enrollment or population figures which may have a different computational base.

Note these are percentage of population or total enrollment to public school course enrollment; private school statistics are not included.

Sources: For 1948/49 - 1970/71 enrollment figures, U.S. Office of Education, Digest of Educational Statistics, 1973 Edition (Washington, D.C., 1974), Table 47, p. 42; for 1972/73, U.S. Office of Education, unpublished data from the 1972/73 survey of school enrollment. Total Population data obtained from U.S. Census of Population 1970, Vol. I., Summary Statistics, Table 51.

CHART 8-1
HIGH SCHOOL ENROLLMENTS IN MATHEMATICS AND
SCIENCE COURSES AS PERCENT OF TOTAL HIGH SCHOOL
ENROLLMENTS, GRADES 7-12, U.S. PUBLIC SCHOOLS,
SELECTED SCHOOL YEARS, 1948/9-1972/3

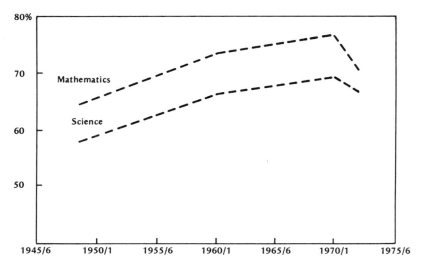

Source: See Table 8-1.

and numerical attendance figures, plus the changing size of the
total age group population. Table 8-2 also includes a division of
the data into public and private school statistics, with the private
school science participation rate estimated by projecting the
public school proportions.

Combining the data from Tables 8-1 and 8-2, Chart 8-2 displays
the historical trend in science course enrollment from 1890 to
1973. The data from Table 8-2 are displayed as a historical trend in
Chart 8-2 from *1890-1965*.

It is evident from the historical trend data that there was a very
large growth in the absolute numbers of high school students
and in science course enrollments. Over this long period, the
proportion of the age group population attending high school
grew from less than 10 percent to over 90 percent. Enrollments in
high school science courses grew more or less as rapidly as high
school enrollments at various times, but, over the long run,

190

TABLE 8-2

HIGH SCHOOL AGE POPULATION, SCHOOL ENROLLMENT AND SCIENCE COURSE ENROLLMENT, 1890-1965

Year	Population (Ages:14-17)	Total Enrollment Public (Private)	Total (Grades 9-12)	Science Enrollment Public (Private)	Total	Percent in Science % Pop.	% Enroll.	Math Enrollment Public (Private)	Total	Percent in Math % Pop.	% Enroll.
1890	5,354,653	202,963* (94,931)*	359,949	66,687 (31,191)	97,878	1.83	27.19	135,444 (63,351)	198,795	3.71	55.23
1900	6,152,231	519,251* (110,793)*	699,403	435,844 (93,000)	528,844	8.60	75.61	464,437 (74,833)	539,240	8.75	77.10
1910	7,220,298	915,061* (117,400)*	1,115,398	603,314 (77,404)	680,718	9.43	61.03	662,189 (84,957)	747,146	10.35	66.98
1915	7,619,600	1,456,000 (155,000)	1,611,000	765,498 (81,492)	846,990	11.12	52.58	895,818 (95,365)	991,183	13.01	61.53
1922	8,260,000	2,873,000 (226,000)	3,099,000	1,256,922 (96,890)	1,355,812	16.41	43.75	1,654,158 (130,174)	1,784,312	21.60	57.58
1928	9,213,000	3,911,000 (269,000)	4,180,000	1,530,419 (105,213)	1,635,632	17.75	39.13	1,854,077 (127,524)	1,981,601	21.51	47.41
1934	9,526,000	5,669,000 (270,000)	5,939,000	2,306,126 (109,835)	2,415,961	25.36	40.68	2,527,587 (120,382)	2,647,969	22.50	44.59
1949	8,622,884	5,717,000 (662,000)	6,379,000	2,915,672 (336,810)	3,252,482	37.71	50.91	2,955,539 (342,237)	3,297,776	38.24	51.70
1961	11,576,439	9,074,000 (1,110,000)	10,184,000	4,902,967 (599,768)	5,502,735	47.53	54.03	5,155,575 (630,669)	5,786,244	49.98	56.82
1965	13,792,500	11,296,672 (1,341,488)	12,638,160	7,243,600 (860,183)	8,103,783	58.75	64.12	7,496,300 (890,119)	8,386,419	60.80	66.36

*Excludes enrollment in subcollegiate departments of institutions of higher education and in residential schools for exceptional children.

Population and Total Enrollment for years 1890, 1900, 1910, 1949, 1961, and 1965 were obtained from Digest of Educational Statistics 1973, Table 33, p. 33. The other years were obtained from communications with the Office of Education.

The number of people enrolled in Science and Math courses in grades 9-12 was obtained from Office of Education, Subject Offerings and Enrollments in Public Secondary Schools, Table 7, p. 99, 1965.

Enrollments in Science and Math courses in private schools were estimated by the formula: Subject Enrollment = Total Private Enroll. x $\dfrac{\text{Subj. Enroll in Public School}}{\text{Total Public School Enroll.}}$

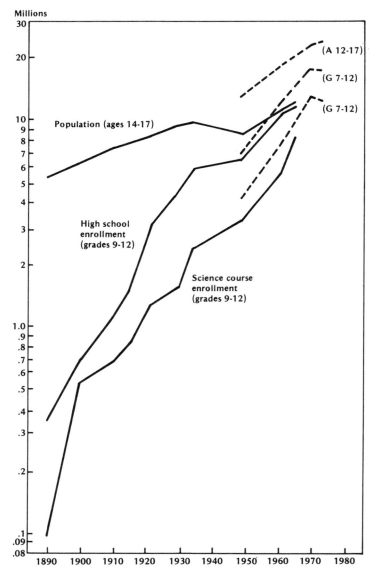

Source: See Tables 8-1 and 8-2.

science course enrollments increased at a faster rate than total high school enrollments. This rapid growth in science course enrollments ended at some point around 1970, when enrollments in the courses declined absolutely as well as relative to high school enrollments, as Chart 8-2 depicts. (Note that, given the discrete nature of the observations, one cannot be certain of the exact point in time between 1962 and 1970 that the downturn actually began.)

**Indicators of Science
Learning: Levels of Science Knowledge**

In deciding to explore performance trends in science among 17-year-olds (this age group was chosen on the basis of availability of data and because that age is close to the end of the high school cycle), it is necessary to address the issue of what the specific indicators of knowledge level are. Unlike course enrollment, which has straightforward measurements, indicators of science performance involve more complex requirements and issues. An indicator or indicators of national science "performance" level should fulfill the following criteria: (1) be national in scope without representing any one region or class out of proportion to its national position; (2) give some indication of the overall level of *general* science knowledge and not some subject of scientific knowledge; (3) give reasonable indication of the general "performance" trend in science over time; (4) provide some feeling for the shape of the distribution of performance at both a static time point and, if possible, along some temporal path; and (5) correlate fairly well with other indicators of science knowledge.

In an attempt to fulfill these desiderata, we turned to the various standardized tests of science knowledge. These tests or studies represent national evaluations, in some examples even over time, of science knowledge at the general level. From such tests, we extracted two indicators: (1) the average score of the general science performance level of 17-year-olds; and (2) the cumulative and frequency distribution of these high school science achievement scores.

There are a number of standardized tests or surveys from which the indicators could have been chosen; our choice, however, only includes the use of the IOWA Test of Educational Development (ITED), Science Subtest,[1] and the National Assessment of

Educational Progress, Science Knowledge.[2] These two works have the important feature of offering not only a measurement of science performance level of 17-year-olds but they also provide these measurements at more than one point in time. The IOWA test has three time points, while the National Assessment offers two points.[3] The time intervals defined by these points overlap somewhat, which permits some rudimentary judgments about the trend in science performance of 17-year-olds for a longer time span.[4]

Test Measurements

We shall now consider some of the findings of these tests. Table 8-3 lists the percentile norms for performance in the second semester of the eleventh grade for high school students on science knowledge tests for 1962 and 1971. Chart 8-3 shows

TABLE 8-3

PERCENTILE NORMS OF PERFORMANCE IN SCIENCE TESTS
FOR SECOND SEMESTER 11TH GRADERS, 1971 AND 1962

Standard Scores	Percentile Ranks of Standard Scores		Standard Scores	Percentile Ranks of Standard Scores	
	1971	1962		1971	1962
35	--	--	17	51	58
34	--	--	16	46	53
33	--	--	15	40	47
32	--	--	14	36	42
31	99	99	13	29	38
30	98	98	12	23	33
29	96	97	11	18	28
28	94	96	10	14	24
27	91	94	9	11	19
26	86	92	8	7	14
25	84	89	7	5	10
24	78	86	6	4	7
23	75	82	5	2	6
22	71	79	4	2	4
21	68	75	3	1	3
20	65	72	2	--	2
19	60	68	1	--	1
18	56	63			

Source: ITED Norm Summaries, 1971 and 1962, p. 5, Table V for 1971 summaries and p. 13 for 1962 summaries.

CHART 8-3
CUMULATIVE PERFORMANCE DISTRIBUTIONS, 1971 AND 1962, OF THE IOWA TEST OF EDUCATIONAL DEVELOPMENT (ITED)

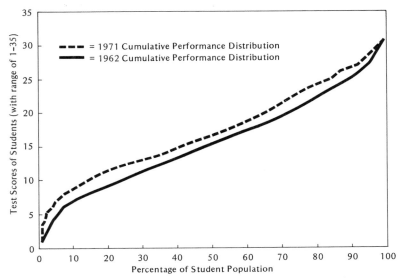

Source: 1962 and 1971 IOWA Test of Educational Development Norms and Conversion Tables, pp. 5 and 13.

visually what the two resultant cumulative distributions look like. (Similar information for the 1957 test is not available.) Chart 8-4 shows the frequency distributions for the two time periods.

As Table 8-3 and Charts 8-3 and 8-4 emphasize, between 1962 and 1971 there was a general increase in the level of science knowledge by 17-year-olds. To investigate the observed increase, we decided to look also at the change in mean performance scores over the longer period, 1957 to 1971. The curve in Chart 8-5 is a point connected graph of the three norm mean scores in science: 15.6 for 1957, 16.1 for 1962 and 16.7 for 1971 taken from ITED, shown together with the two interpolated performance points from the National Assessment surveys (see Table 8-4).

Over the 14-year period from 1957 to 1971, there was a definite, although slight, increasing trend. Such trend information suggests that during this period, programmatically through either increased funding of science education and/or an improvement of the efficiency of science teachers, students were gaining a bit more science knowledge. Conversely, this performance increase

195

CHART 8-4

PERFORMANCE FREQUENCY DISTRIBUTION, 1971 AND 1962,
OF THE IOWA TEST OF EDUCATIONAL DEVELOPMENT (ITED)

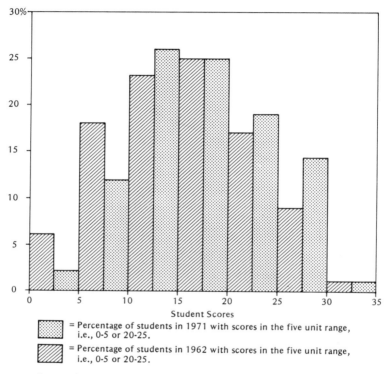

Student Scores

= Percentage of students in 1971 with scores in the five unit range,
i.e., 0-5 or 20-25.

= Percentage of students in 1962 with scores in the five unit range,
i.e., 0-5 or 20-25.

Source: Same as Table 8-3.

could indicate more science knowledge absolutely by students
due to greater interest in science or availability of information
from nonschool sources. Given the very public scientific
achievements and problems of the 1950s and '60s, such change in
student interest or exposure to science information is quite
possible.

However, if we turn to the National Assessment information, a
different picture emerges for 1969 and 1973. In 1969, the percentage of correctly answered science questions (note that NAEP
does not employ the achievement test's scoring system) was
about 44.2 percent. The early results from the 1972/73 second

196

CHART 8-5

MEAN SCORES IN THE IOWA TEST OF EDUCATION AND DEVELOPMENT (ITED) AND THE NATIONAL ASSESSMENT OF EDUCATIONAL PROGRESS (NAEP) PERCENTAGE CORRECT FOR 17-YEAR-OLDS

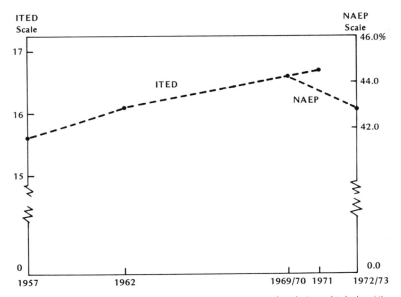

Note: Scales have been aligned so that the NAEP score for 1969/70 corresponds to the interpolated value of the ITED score for the same year.

Source: See Table 8-4.

evaluation suggests the percentage of "correctly answered or completed tasks" declined by about 1.4 percent[5] or to a correctly answered level of 42.8 percent. Of course, the question must be raised: do these two results contradict each other? Why was there a 7 percent increase over a 14-year period and then a 1.4 percent decline in a 4-year period?

Trend Analysis

During the late 1950s, there was a tremendous increase in the resources allocated for science curriculum improvements and general science-related program creation. This increase may have reflected a growing national concern over an apparent lag in science performance as compared to other nations. The great infusion of funds continued until recently. Quite possibly the

TABLE 8-4

MEAN SCORES IN THE IOWA TEST OF
EDUCATIONAL DEVELOPMENT (ITED)
FOR 11TH GRADERS AND THE NATIONAL
ASSESSMENT OF EDUCATIONAL PROGRESS
(NAEP) PERCENTAGE CORRECT FOR ALL
17 YEAR OLDS

MEAN SCORES IN ITED FOR
11TH GRADERS

Year	Science Mean Score
1957 *	15.6
1962	16.1
1971	16.7

NAEP PERCENTAGE CORRECT FOR
17 YEAR OLDS

Year	Percentage Correct
1969/70 **	44.2%
1972/73	42.8

*These ITED mean scores are for tests given in the last
month of the second semester of the 11th grade.

**NAEP examinations were given throughout the year.

Though NAEP science survey was for all 17-year olds both in and
out of school, those scores are only for in-school respondents.

Sources: IOWA Tests of Education Development--A Summary of
Changes in the ITED Norms (Iowa: The University of Iowa, 1971);
National Assessment of Educational Progress, Report #1, 1969-
1970, Science: National Results (Denver: Education Commission
of the States, 1970); National Assessment of Science, 1969-1973,
Science Report No. 04-5-00 (Washington, D.C.: U.S. Government
Printing Office, February 1975), p. 3; and The Condition of Educa-
tion: A Statistical Report on the Condition of American Education
(Washington, D.C.: NAEP, 1975), p. 137, Table 14.

early trend increases were a response to this increased emphasis on education in general and science in particular. By the late 1960s, the general level of interest in science may have diminished and the result would be reflected in the classroom. Also though, by the late 1960s and early '70s, the effect of the initial surge in performance may have stabilized and possibly a slight decline should have been expected as a new plateau was reached.

As further evidence of an interest drop rather than a decline in the efficiency of teaching science, we return to the enrollment in science course tables and graphs. As we noted from both Tables 8-1 and 8-2, the enrollment in science courses definitely declined. Since the National Assessment tests were a survey of 17-year-olds both in and out of school and not only those in school and enrolled in science courses, a simple decline in enrollment would be reflected in any survey of the entire age group.[6] Whereas up until the mid-1960s, science was often a required subject in most curriculums, after that time a large proportion of the curriculum was elective and the attendance in science courses would be a more direct indicator of student interest rather than administrative decision or direction.

Another line of thinking could lead to the following scenario: there exists a high correlation between performance in reading skills and performance in all other courses, including science. The slight decline in science performance may reflect a deficiency in reading rather than a cause directly related to the science program.

Conclusion

In spite of the reservations and cautions that must be voiced in attempting to interpret the evidence, it appears reasonable to conclude that during most of the 1960s there was a positive change in the level of science knowledge performance by 17-year-olds. Also, by the end of the 1960s and early '70s, two events were occurring: first, a decline in enrollment in science (and math) courses both absolutely and relative to the total student enrollment; and second, a shift from growth to a decrease in the level of science knowledge. The exact nature of the decline in either enrollment or performance cannot be conclusively explained given the absence of more supporting evidence.

Notes

1 *IOWA Tests of Educational Development Norms and Conversion Tables* (Chicago: Science Research Associates, Inc., 1963), p. 13; *IOWA Tests of Educational Development—A Summary of Changes in the ITED Norms* (Iowa: The University of Iowa, 1971), pp. 1, 5; and *1971 Standardization Norms: National Percentiles for the IOWA Tests of Educational Development* (Chicago: Science Research Associates, 1971), p. 11. The ITED distribution and norm figures are grade based as opposed to age-group based. The grade figures are for second semester eleventh graders.

2 See *National Assessment of Educational Progress, Report No. 1, 1969-1970, Science: National Results* (Denver: Education Commission of the States, 1970); ibid., *Report No. 7, Science: Group and Balanced Group Results* (1973), pp. 160-178; and *National Assessments of Science, 1969 and 1973* (Denver: Education Commission of the States, 1975), pp. 3, 4.

3 Even though the ITED is a test popular primarily in the Midwest and Southwest, the sample population from which its normalizing time tests were taken was a national sample. This sample procedure thus avoided the problem of test calibration using only customers, which would have resulted in a biased set of norm tables.

4 Reviewing the history of these two tests, we consider first the ITED. The IOWA Test of Educational Development (ITED) originally was developed at the State University of Iowa and is now produced by Science Research Associates. The ITED represents a series of national norm-setting tests given in 1957, 1962 and 1971. These norm tests are one of the few longitudinal measurements which employed the same score scale of science knowledge of 17-year-olds at each time point. This score scale has a range from 1 to 35. The substance of the tests consists of achievement questions of the multiple-choice variety. Some comparability over time is possible since some questions are repeated at all three time points.

The National Assessment of Educational Progress, Science Knowledge, was given in 1969/1970 and 1972/1973 to a national sample of 17-year-olds. (Actually, tests were also given to three other age groups: 9-year-olds, 13-year-olds and "young adult," 26- to 35-year-olds.) Unlike the ITED, the National Assessment tests are not exactly achievement-oriented tests, but rather represent a task-oriented evaluation of an age group. Here, students are often asked to complete or perform some experiment or demonstration, i.e., properly balance a scale, identify leaf shapes or complete a graph.

The National Assessment studies in science are part of a major effort begun in 1964 via the Education Commission of the States to produce reliable national evaluations of performance levels of basic education for youths and young adults.

5 For the entire sample of 17-year-olds, both in or out of school, the decline was 2.3 percent instead of 1.4 percent.

6 As added evidence, note the greater decline registered when both in-school and out-of-school respondents are considered: 2.3 percent versus 1.4 percent.